Ultimate Sex ♥

For several years we have spoken to young people about love, sex and dating. Almost every place we go, we ask people to write down their questions about sex. The same questions appear again and again.

Is sex dirty?
Why are guys so weird?
Why are girls so strange?
Why wait for sex?
What if I'm pressured?
How far is too far?
Is lust abnormal?
What about masturbation?
How do I handle sexual problems?
We're pregnant — what do we do?
How do I straighten out the past?
How do I get control?

These are hard questions — the answers are hard, too. The easy part is knowing what is right and wrong in handling sex. The hard part is bringing your life in line before you get married so that you can enjoy the very best in sex after you get married.

The purpose of this book is to answer your hard questions about sex and to give practical solutions to everyone who desires the best sexually.

Here's Life Books

Desiring the Best

Barry St. Clair & Bill Jones

Here's Life Publishers

FIRST PRINTING, NOVEMBER 1987
SECOND PRINTING, JUNE 1988

Published by
HERE'S LIFE PUBLISHERS, INC.
P.O. Box 1576
San Bernardino, CA 92402

HLP Product Number 951988

Library of Congress Cataloging-in-Publication Data

St. Clair, Barry
    Sex, desiring the best.

    Includes bibliographies.
    1. Sexual ethics for youth. 2. Sex instructions for youth — United States — Religious aspects —
Christianity. 3. Youth — United States — Sexual behavior.
I. Jones, Bill, 1955-   . II. Title.
HQ35.S725   1987   306.7'088055   87-26172

ISBN 0-89840-196-8 (pbk.)

Unless otherwise indicated, Scripture quotations are from *The Holy Bible, New International Version*, © 1978 by New York International Bible Society, published by the Zondervan Corporation, Grand Rapids, Michigan.

Scripture quotations designated NASB are from *The New American Standard Bible*, © The Lockman Foundation 1960, 1962, 1963, 1968, 1971, 1972, 1975, 1977.

Scripture quotations designated TLB are from *The Living Bible*, © 1971 by Tyndale House Publishers, Wheaton, Illinois.

Scripture quotations designated KJV are from the *King James Version* of the Bible.

Scripture quotations designated RSV are from *The Revised Standard Version* © 1952 Thomas Nelson & Sons, New York, New York.

FOR MORE INFORMATION, WRITE:

L.I.F.E. — P.O. Box A399, Sydney South 2000, Australia
Campus Crusade for Christ of Canada — Box 300, Vancouver, B.C. V6C 2X3, Canada
Campus Crusade for Christ — Pearl Assurance House, 4 Temple Row, Birmingham, B2 5HG, England
Lay Institute for Evangelism — P.O. Box 8786, Auckland 3, New Zealand
Campus Crusade for Christ — P.O. Box 240, Colombo Court Post Office, Singapore 9117
Great Commission Movement of Nigeria — P.O. Box 500, Jos, Plateau State Nigeria, West Africa
Campus Crusade for Christ International — Arrowhead Springs, San Bernardino, CA 92414, U.S.A.
Reach Out Ministries — 120 N. Avondale Road, Avondale Estates, GA 30002
Student Mission Impact — P. O. Box 2200, Stone Mountain, GA 30086

*Dedicated to
those students around the world
who have committed themselves
to waiting for God's best*

Contents

God Has a Plan!

Can you believe it? God has a plan for your sex life! And this book can show you what that plan is.

Being your age today isn't easy. Sex is everywhere—in your music and magazines, on TV and at the movies, at the parties you go to, on the posters you buy, the calendars you look at, in the jokes you hear. At times it seems like everyone is doing it with everybody.

But God didn't plan it that way. He created sex to be a very unique and very special act — the culmination of the marriage commitment between *a* man and *a* woman.

Barry and Bill, in their up-front and up-beat style, will help you discover God's plan for your sex life. They've addressed the twelve questions that the young people they come in contact with keep on asking. And they've pulled no punches.

You'll get straight talk about lust and masturbation. You'll find help in dealing with unwanted pregnancy, rape and incest. Maybe you have a problem with homosexuality or pornography. A lot of you have messed around with sexual intercourse and now want to get your life straightened out. Perhaps you're under pressure from your boyfriend or girlfriend to give in sexually. You might have problems keeping your thought life under control. Maybe you're a virgin, and you're terrified that you're the last one on earth. You've wondered, *What's the use of waiting anyway?*

Barry and Bill understand. Let their insights and wisdom from God's Word guide you in your decisions concerning your sex life. They've put the answers right here. This is by far one of the best books on sexual values for young men and women that I've ever seen.

God cares about you. He wants your sex life to be

great, terrific, fantastic, awesome . . . and He has a plan!
Trust Him with this area of your life. You want the best —
God's got it!

Josh McDowell
Series Editor

A Special Thanks

To Chris Frear for editing and advice.

To Gina Dixon for typing the manuscript many times.

To Fran Stephens for correcting the manuscript.

To the Bowers and Douglases for reading the book from a parent's perspective and giving input.

To Josh and Dottie McDowell and the Here's Life staff for their enthusiasm, support and help.

To our wives and families who gave up precious time with us in order that we might communicate the significant message of this book.

To the Lord Jesus for His guidance on what to say and how to say it from the beginning to the end.

The Golden Locket

A Short Parable About Sex (For Those Who Can't Wait)

by Bob Wolgemuth

Three dates, a string of hurried cafeteria lunches together, countless rushed snatches of conversation in the halls between classes, and Matt knew he was in love.

That's why he was wandering around downtown for three hours the Saturday before Christmas. He had searched everywhere for the perfect gift, but nothing seemed quite right for Carrie.

He finally sauntered into a jewelry store. After a few awkward minutes of looking, he explained to the saleslady he wanted a really nice present for his girlfriend.

She told him she thought she had just the thing and led Matt to a nearby brown velvet box, set it in front of Matt and waited for his reaction.

The moment he opened the box and saw that gold locket, Matt knew it was perfect. The gold glistened in the light — just like Carrie's eyes. The quality of the locket was obvious, even without the "24K" tag. The 14K gold chain added a touch of elegance. It was expensive, but Matt had been saving a long time. And he knew Carrie couldn't help but love it. So he paid for it, took it home, and very carefully wrapped it himself.

That locket did make the perfect gift. Carrie thought so too. And Matt knew as long as he lived, he'd never forget the night he gave Carrie that gold locket.

Winter hadn't reached February before something happened to Matt's love. The warmth seemed to fade. Matt knew Carrie sensed it; he could see the questions in her eyes. Breaking up brought the greatest sense of sadness and loss

Matt had ever known.

A few months later Matt met Rita. She was just the opposite of Carrie, with dark, flashing eyes and a fiery personality. Love struck again. And Matt decided he wanted to show his love for Rita with a special gift.

He haunted stores trying to decide what to buy. But he always found himself back in the jewelry store looking at the gold lockets. He racked his brain for other ideas, but no other gift seemed as perfect.

He ended up giving Rita a locket — just like the one he had given to Carrie. She thought it was beautiful and Matt was pleased with his selection.

Matt and Rita broke up a few months later. After Rita, he dated Barb, and after Barb came Sandy and Arlene and then Nicole. There was nothing strange about the fact that Matt went through a string of girlfriends. He really cared about each one.

But it did seem odd, even to Matt, that whenever a birthday or some other special occasion called for a special gift, he would return to the familiar jewelry store to buy another gold locket. A couple of times he felt a little guilty about not putting any more thought or effort into choosing a gift. But even when he tried, he couldn't think of a nicer present than that locket.

Finally Matt met Melissa. Right away there was a different look about him when he was with her; he acted calmer, more sure of himself. He knew that no one had ever understood or loved him the way Melissa did. All his previous loves paled in the light of his love for Melissa. No one was surprised when Matt asked her to marry him.

A few weeks before the wedding, Melissa suggested they exchange wedding gifts. Matt thought that was a great idea. He wanted this gift to be just as special as the wedding rings they'd picked out together — and just as symbolic of his love.

He tried to think of something else, but he finally settled on that beautiful, gold locket. He went to pick it up at the same jewelry store, and the moment he saw it, he remembered just what a perfect gift it was. Nothing else seemed to express his love quite the way that locket did.

Their wedding was as exciting and beautiful as both Matt and Melissa had dreamed. And when the exhausting day of ceremony and festivity came to a close, and the two of them were finally alone, Matt presented his gift to Melissa.

She told him the locket was beautiful. She also said she loved him and that he'd given her the happiest day and most wonderful gift she'd ever had.

But when Melissa put on the locket, Matt couldn't help remembering all the other gold lockets he'd given. He wished he could have given her something truly unique, for her alone.

Always before, that 24K gold locket had seemed such a perfect gift. But now, on the happiest day of his life, that locket didn't seem special or beautiful anymore. It didn't even look as gold as Matt remembered.

Reprinted with permission from Campus Life *magazine, Christianity Today, Inc., 1978.*

Introduction

Sex.

Now you're waiting for the next word. We've got your attention. Just that short, three-letter word grabs your interest. Why? Not because of what it *says*, but what it *suggests*.

You, like everyone else, are interested in sex. That's because you are a sexual person with sexual desires. But the bigger issue is, *What are you going to do with your sexuality?*

Sex can be . . .

    wonderful or horrible
    beautiful or ugly
    exciting or scary

depending on how you use it.

According to recent statistics, "American girls, on the average, begin having sex at age 16; boys at 15.5. By the end of their teens, 70 percent of girls and 80 percent of boys have been sexually active. Every year, 1 million adolescent girls become pregnant. About 400,000 have abortions. Of those who give birth, half are not yet eighteen."[1] You can see that most students are not handling their sexuality well.

If sex consumes you, if you have not gotten into it at all, or if you're somewhere in between, this book will answer your questions because it addresses those questions asked most by young people. We believe it will not only help you to understand your sexuality, but will also challenge you to reach your highest sexual potential.

Barry St. Clair
Reach Out Ministries
120 N. Avondale Road
Avondale Estates, GA 30002

Bill Jones
Student Mission Impact
P.O. Box 2200
Stone Mountain, GA 30086

1

Is Sex Dirty? ♥

*O*ne day I walked into the library, expecting to study," Barry recalls from college, "but when I looked to my left, I saw the most beautiful girl ever. I stopped and stared at her through the stacks of books. I had to meet her! One problem, though — sitting next to her was her date. So I collected my courage, walked over and started talking to her date.

"Of course, he introduced me to her. We started talking, and kept talking and talking and talking. I'm not sure what happened to her date. He may still be in the library! All I could think about was *Carol Price*.

"The next night I asked her out for a study date. (That's when you go to the library and leave your books, then go out and have fun!) Again we talked and talked. What a lady! The relationship was really rolling!

"One year later, on June 14, we walked down the

aisle and said 'I do.' After she tossed her bouquet, we drove
to our honeymoon hotel. I carried her across the threshold,
closed the door, and . . . WOW!

"Seventeen years and four children later, I can assure
you — sex is great!

"It's terrific!

"Awesome!

"Fantastic!

"And I'll bet you want to be in on it too!"

WHY THE EXCITEMENT?

Fantastic sex is sex the way God created it.   God
designed sex to be exciting and awesome, beautiful and intimate.   In fact, God is more excited about sex than we are, or
ever will be.

Sound weird?   God excited about sex?   Maybe you
think He's not at all fired up about it.   Maybe you even think
He's down on it.   No way. The Bible is never down on the
use of sex, but on the *misuse* of sex outside a loving commitment between a husband and wife.

No matter where you look — billboards, magazines,
movies, TV, videos — you see sex.   You don't see fantastic
sex, though.   What you see is sick sex — sex outside of
God's plan.   Sick sex expresses itself in two opposite ways.

Sex is evil. "Sex is bad.   Sex is wrong. But it is
necessary to have children.   Whatever you do, *don't* enjoy
it."

Sex — anytime, anyplace, with anybody. "Sex is like
eating a hamburger and drinking a Coke — no big deal.   So
'do it' anytime you want.   Give free expression to your sexual drives.   Enjoy it with anybody — whoever turns you on
at the time."

God is not excited about sick sex. He is, however,
fired up about people using their sexuality the way He created it. That's what 1 Corinthians 6:13 says: "The body is
not meant for sexual immorality, but for the Lord, and the
Lord for the body." Your body wasn't designed for sick sex.
God designed your sexuality. It is a gift He has given you,

and He knows how to help you use that gift best.

Suppose we design and build an expensive, incredibly accurate watch for you, and we give it to you as a gift. It's just what you need and want. It looks perfect on you. Along with it, we give you a book that describes exactly how to use it and care for it. What a neat gift!

In the same way, God is the "body designer." He made your body and has given it to you as a gift. Your sexual desires have been designed by God. He created male and female — men and women — in His image (just like Him). And what is the first thing He told them to do? Have sex! Isn't that what He says? "Be fruitful and increase in number; fill the earth" (Genesis 1:28). God designed only one way to multiply, and that's to have kids. And He designed only one way to have kids, and that's to have sexual intercourse.

Then what did God do? Did He say, "Sex is dirty," or "Sex is free; it doesn't harm anything, so do it with anybody you please"? Not a chance. Genesis 1:31 says, "God saw all that he had made, and it was very good." Sex came directly from God's heart. It is important and good. Sex in itself is never bad — it can only be used wrongly.

Do you follow what we're saying? All that God creates and gives is good. *And God gave you your sexual desires!*

A lovely young lady wrote about her bridegroom in the Song of Solomon:

"My lover is radiant and ruddy, outstanding among ten thousand. His head is purest gold; his hair is wavy and black as a raven. His eyes are like doves by the water streams, washed in milk, mounted like jewels."

He is tanned and handsome.

"His cheeks are like beds of spice yielding perfume."

He uses great-smelling aftershave.

"His lips are like lilies dripping with myrrh."

His breath smells great.

"His arms are rods of gold set with chrysolite. His body is like polished ivory decorated with sapphires. His

legs are pillars of marble set on bases of pure gold.   His
appearance is like Lebanon, choice as its cedars" (Song of
Songs 5:10-15).

He has a gorgeous body.

Now read what this handsome hunk has to say about
his bride in the same book (Song of Songs 7:1-9):

"How beautiful your sandaled feet, O prince's
daughter! Your graceful legs are like jewels, the work of a
craftsman hands."

Great legs.

"Your navel is a rounded goblet that never lacks
blended wine.   Your waist is a mound of wheat encircled by
lilies."

What a body!

"Your breasts are like two fawns, twins of a gazelle."

Wow!

"Your neck is like an ivory tower.   Your eyes are the
pools of Heshbon by the gate of Bath Rabbim."

(He's checking out every part.)

"Your nose is like the tower of Lebanon looking toward Damascus."

(Oops!   He got carried away.)

"Your head crowns you like Mount Carmel.   Your
hair is like royal tapestry; the king is held captive by its
tresses."

A terrific face.

"How beautiful you are and how pleasing, O love,
with your delights!"

A knock-out — 10-plus!

"Your stature is like that of the palm, and your
breasts like clusters of fruit."

A perfect figure.

"I said, 'I will climb the palm tree; I will take hold
of its fruit.'   May your breasts be like the clusters of the
vine, the fragrance of your breath like apples, and your
mouth like the best wine."

(And he's enjoying it all!)

That's not a porn magazine.   If you've never been

interested in the Bible, we're sure you're interested now!

When you read that, you have to believe that God is excited about sex. Your sexual desires were given to you by God as a gift. So when your sexual motor revs up to 110 m.p.h., remember that God designed you that way.

WHAT'S THE PLAN?

Not only did God create your sexuality, He has a purpose for it.

Since God designed you to have the most exciting sex life possible, He has given clear instructions on how to use it. He has given you an "owner's manual" — the Bible.

If you decide to accept that elegant watch we created for you, you can choose how to wear it. Say you decide to wear it on your foot and stomp around. One of us would grab you by the nose, look you square in the eye and say, "Stop! You'll crack the crystal and ruin the watch. Read the owner's manual."

That's not *exactly* how God would handle it, but if you use sex incorrectly, God wants to stop you and get you to follow the instructions in your owner's manual — the Bible. Why? For your *protection* (that's why He stops you) and for your *provision* (that's why He points you to the owner's manual). His protection and provision are an expression of His love for you.

Reasons for Sex

• *To have babies.* That's how we all got here. It is a proven fact that if your parents didn't have children, you won't either. So it's not a bad reason at all.

• *To enjoy pleasure.* Sex is fun! No argument about that.

• *To express love.* Sex can be the most intimate way to say, "I love you." And all of us want to express love.

All of these are good reasons to have sex. But God has something better in mind.

If we go back in history over 4000 years, we find

that one of the greatest leaders of all time, Moses, made this statement: "For this reason a man will leave his father and mother and be united to his wife, and they will become one flesh" (Genesis 2:24).

Then 2000 years ago the Greatest Man Who Ever Lived — Jesus — said, "Haven't you read . . . that at the beginning the Creator 'made them male and female,' and said 'For this reason a man will leave his father and mother and be united to his wife, and the two will become one flesh'? So they are no longer two, but one. Therefore, what God has joined together, let man not separate" (Matthew 19:4-6).

Several years later one of the world's greatest thinkers, the apostle Paul, wrote a letter to the Christians in the city of Corinth. In Corinth they had a temple to Aphrodite, the goddess of sex. People would go to the temple of Aphrodite and have sex with the prostitutes. Paul gives instructions to the Christians who were going over to the temple after church for a little "after-church fellowship." He tells them: "Do you not know that he who unites himself with a prostitute is one with her in body? For it is said, 'The two will become one flesh'" (1 Corinthians 6:16).

Obviously if Moses, Jesus and Paul put the same instructions in the "owner's manual," then that message is important. What does it mean?

Total Dynamic Oneness

God designed sex to unite two people in marriage. Although people can have sex to have babies, to feel pleasure and to show love, God's higher plan is for *total dynamic oneness*. And that can happen *only in marriage*.

One student asked us, "Why do people make such a big deal out of intercourse?" The answer: The Bible teaches that it is more than merely a physical act when two people have sex. They become "one flesh." Both give themselves to each other. They become one person. How?

Sex joins personalities. When you have sexual intercourse with another person, you join your personality with that other person's personality. It's more than the TV, movies and magazines portray it — "Do it. You'll love it." So you see Bob walk up to Jane and say, "Hi, I'm Bob. Will you go to bed with me?" And Jane says, "Bob, I'd love to go to bed with you!" They get into the car and drive into the sunset.

God didn't intend sex for the back seat of a car. When the Bible says, "A man shall leave . . . and cleave" (Matthew 19:5), it means to glue, to cement. A man and woman in sexual intercourse cement their personalities together. If you have sex and then break up with that person, you have left a part of your personality behind and torn away some of the other person's personality as well. Both of you are hurt and incomplete.

It takes more than sex to experience the total dynamic oneness of marriage. "One flesh" means that two people establish a relationship and become companions on every level — spiritual, mental, emotional. Then, and only then, does the physical take on deep significance. Here's a simple picture of what it looks like to help you grasp the concept of a total relationship:

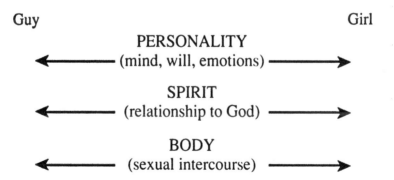

Guy   Girl

PERSONALITY
◄——————— (mind, will, emotions) ———————►

SPIRIT
◄——————— (relationship to God) ———————►

BODY
◄——————— (sexual intercourse) ———————►

This is one of the main reasons God designed marriage — to bring two people together as "one flesh."

When a couple has sexual intercourse, they enter into the most private, personal relationship possible. Both people reveal the most intimate parts of themselves to each other. God preserves that for marriage. Only in marriage is there enough trust and confidence in the other person's commitment; you can really be yourself and let the other person know who you are. Sex is the ultimate expression of this trust. That is total dynamic oneness.

This diagram shows you the proper emphasis in building toward total dynamic oneness in marriage:

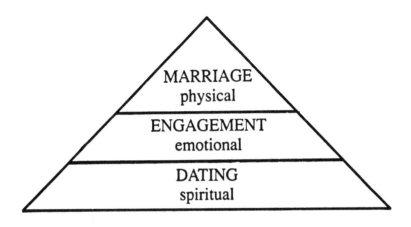

But that's not the approach of many students today. On the first date a couple gets to know each other and ends their evening with a vacuum-cleaner, good night kiss. The second date ends in a wrestling match. The third date they go all the way. Now they have nothing new to look forward to. They get into this mess because they think, "If I can just please the other person physically, if we just get it together sexually, we can solve any problem." That's a lie. In a few days or weeks they will experience guilt, disappointment and heartache. That's not God's way.

This all-too-common approach looks like this:

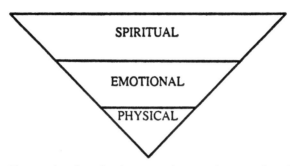

From simple physics you know that a triangle can't stand on its tip. It's doomed to come crashing down. Making the physical aspect the foundation of your relationship will lead to destruction.

Following the first diagram will make your relationships the best, so at the right time you will be sexually prepared for marriage.

In *dating* you concentrate on your *spiritual growth* — sharing your love for God and others.

In *engagement* you develop an *emotional oneness* by opening your hearts to each other, sharing your heart's secrets.

In *marriage* you *become one physically*, expressing the most intimate relationship possible. If the physical comes first, you have total disaster, not total dynamic oneness. But with the foundation of the spiritual, and the support of the emotional, a relationship grows into total dynamic oneness. That is God's exciting plan for your sex life.

WHO OWNS YOUR BODY?

So what do you do between now and marriage?

Well, God has designed sex so it will bring either happiness or heartache, depending on the way you handle your body. And the way you handle your body will be determined by the way you answer this question: *Who owns your body?*

Look at 1 Corinthians 6:19,20: "Do you not know that your body is a temple of the Holy Spirit, who is in you, whom you have received from God? You are not your own; you were bought at a price. Therefore honor God with your body."

Let's go back to the watch illustration. We have given you this expensive, valuable watch as a gift. We have asked you to read the manual. But only *you* can make the choice whether to wear it on your foot, stomp on it and break it, or to wear it on your wrist and let it accomplish its purpose.

Your sex life is the same — you can make only one of two decisions. You can try to own your body and use it wrongly, ruining the precious gift God has given you. Or you can let Jesus own your body and use your special gift in your marriage which will bring dynamic oneness to your relationship, happiness to you and glory to God.

If you decide that *you* want to own your body, the Bible is clear about what the results will be:

For the guys — "But a man who commits adultery lacks judgement; whoever does so destroys himself" (Proverbs 6:32).

For the girls — "For the lips of an adulteress drip honey, and her speech is smoother than oil; but in the end she is bitter as gall, sharp as a double-edged sword. Her feet go down to death" (Proverbs 5:3-5).

You will destroy your life!

But if you let *Jesus Christ* own your body, the results are just as clear. First Corinthians 6:19 says that you were "bought with a price." Your body is precious to Him. When God owns your body He can keep your powerful sexual desires under His control. Sometimes you may feel like there is no way to get your body under control. When you become a believer in Jesus Christ, though, He comes to live in you (that's what 1 Corinthians 6:19 means when it says that "your body is the temple of the Holy Spirit within you") and through Jesus Christ living in you, you have the power to control your sexual desires until you get married.

The opportunity to misuse your sexuality is everywhere. Between now and the time you marry you will have many opportunities to wipe out sexually. In the middle of any of those heavy temptations it will be too late to decide who owns your body. *You must decide now.*

If you want Jesus to own your body, pray this prayer — out loud — right now:

Jesus, I thank you for my body. I'm glad my body is precious to You. I confess that I have owned it myself. That's wrong. Please forgive me. Now I want You to own it. I give my body to You. I invite You into my life to take control so I can have the strength and power to control my sex drives. Use my body for Your glory. In Jesus' name, Amen.

Continue to ask Jesus to control your body every day as you wait for that great, terrific, awesome, fantastic day — your wedding day.

ACTION SECTION

1. In your own words, write why you think God created sex and why He is excited about it.

_____

_____

_____

2. Honestly tell how you feel about your own sex life now.

_____

_____

_____

3. Study 1 Corinthians 6:19,20. Tell why you think God wants to own your body.

_____

_____

4.   Answer this very important question: Who owns your body? ———— I own it. ———— Jesus owns it. How do you know?

_____

_____

_____

5.   What specific steps do you need to take now, in your dating, to prepare for total dynamic oneness in the future?

(1) _____

(2) _____

(3) _____

2

Why Are Guys So Weird? ♥

*G*irls, how many times have you asked yourselves:
  • Why are guys so sexually aggressive?
  • Why are they always after my body?
  • Why can't they keep their hands to themselves?
  • Are all guys sex maniacs?
  • Do they ever think about anything else?
  • Is there even one guy who thinks about any-
    thing other than sex?

You may have your own answers like, "They have big heads," or "They have ego problems," or "They have a hormone imbalance," or "They think they know everything." Maybe you shrug your shoulders and say with a sigh, "I really don't know."

Well, a fun experiment was conducted with a bunch of guys. They were wired with electrodes attached to a meter that would read their pulse rates. When the guys were shown a picture of a car, their pulse shot up. (Most guys are into cars.) Then they were shown a picture of a flower. Their pulse rates dropped off. (Most guys couldn't care less about flowers.) Then they viewed a picture of a baby. The rates remained about the same. (What's the big deal about a baby?) Then they saw a picture of a naked woman. WWOOONNGG. Their pulses shot right out of the top of the meter. Guys are wired for sex!

WHAT'S THE DIFFERENCE?

Obviously, guys and girls are different.

When you're walking through the mall with your favorite "weird" guy, you want to go in all the dress shops and look at all of the hot new clothes. But he keeps dragging you into the sporting goods stores to show you how to lift weights. Then he takes you into all of the fast food places — and he eats at every one! That's the difference! Or at least an example of the difference.

The Bible explains it this way: God made Adam and then saw that he needed a companion. So God said, "It is not good for the man to be alone. I will make a helper suitable for him" (Genesis 2:18). God made all of these animals and passed each one by Adam to see if one was appealing to him. The giraffe: "She's too tall." The hippo: "She's too fat." The turtle: "Not soft enough." And so on. Adam didn't like any of these, so God caused a deep sleep to come over him. While he slept God took one of his ribs and made a woman. When Adam saw her, his mouth flew open and his pulse rate shot off the meter. He said, "*At last*, this is bone of my bones, flesh of my flesh" (see Genesis 2:21-23). Adam was fired up! This is the companion he needed. Not a relationship like the one with the God he worshiped or like the one with the animals he dominated, but with someone like him — a woman.

But at the same time the woman was like him, she was also different from him. If God had wanted women to be the same as men, He wouldn't have created a woman, He would have just made a copy of Adam. If they had been alike, how boring! Just think how much fun in life we would miss if women were the same as men:

- No dates.
- No romance.
- No conversations with the opposite sex. (Imagine what it would be like never to have talked to a girl or guy.)
- No interesting conversations about the opposite sex. (What would you ever talk about?)
- No perfume or aftershave. (Who would need it?)
- No excitement. (Your friends are one thing, but a cute guy or girl — that's excitement!)
- No one to show off for. (No need for ball games or cheerleading.)
- No marriage. (No one to share your life fully with.)

When God created man and woman He created them to be different — male and female. He was created a *man*. She was created a *woman*. At the moment a baby is born people eagerly ask, "Is it a boy or girl?" From the beginning of life men and women have basic differences, starting with their bodies.

Therefore, sex is not something you do. Sex is part of who you are. Sex is not just the difference in your sex organs and what you do or don't do with them. It's part of your total personality. Everything that touches your body affects your mind, will and emotions and reaches into your spirit. Likewise, what is in your spirit affects how you react with your mind, will and emotions and what you do with your body. Luke 6:45 puts it this way: "The good man brings good things out of the good stored up in his heart, and the evil man brings evil things out of the evil stored up in his heart. For out of the overflow of his heart his mouth speaks." This illustration demonstrates that:

WHAT ARE GUYS LIKE?

You know that God created men and women different from each other. But how is a guy different?

In His Spirit

Although both guys and gals have a "God-shaped vacuum" that can be filled only by Jesus Christ, they respond to that need for God differently.

God made men physically stronger, freer to lead and more aggressive. In other words, *tougher*.

The problem is that without Christ they overemphasize these physical characteristics and they act aggressive, macho, cool — what *every* woman has been waiting for. They're like bricks — hard, rough and abrasive. Instead of attracting girls, they turn them off.

As a guy responds to Christ and the "God-shaped vacuum" is filled, that tough exterior becomes tender. He becomes a velvet-covered brick. And instead of being weak morally and overbearing in personality, he becomes strong with character and convictions, and gentle in personality.

That's the kind of guy you're looking for, isn't it?

In His Personality

In his personality (mind, emotions and will) sex dominates a man more than love does. Josh McDowell says, "I'm convinced sex is dominant in the mind of a man, and love is paramount in the mind of a woman."[1] It's not that girls aren't interested in sex or guys in love. It's a matter of emphasis.

Guys respond more to their basic desires (like hunger, competition, sex). The average guy reacts to a girl on a surface level — "She *looks* great." And his senses feed these basic desires. So, to many guys, a girl is like a pizza — the one that makes his mouth water is the one he wants!

When most guys are attracted to a girl they think first of sex, then of love.

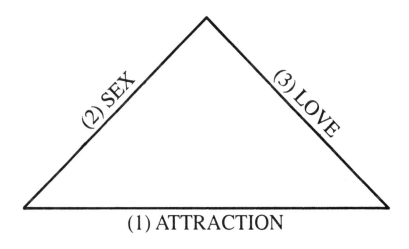

(1) ATTRACTION

Because of their physical make-up, guys have three characteristics that can affect their personality.

They are easily aroused. With one look, guys are at 110 percent. Remember, his senses are directly connected to his desires. Like turning on the motor of a car, he's revved up, ready to go!

When a guy sees a sexy girl, he thinks, "I want her to satisfy me." So he dates this girl. Then he says, "I love her." What he is really saying is, "I love me and I want her." That's because his physical desires dominate his personality. He is easily aroused.

They are easily unaroused. To guys, sex is the release of a bodily desire. Since that sexual desire is so easily aroused and then so quickly satisfied, he can say "I love you," then walk away and say, "I loved it." Just like eating a pizza, the hunger ends.

They are not easily turned back. Guys try to push for more and more sexually. When the girl gives in, the guy finds it difficult to turn back. For example, if he kisses a girl and then fondles her breasts, it's hard for him to go back to "just kissing."

In His Body

That male spirit and personality are connected to a body wired for sex. The main sex organs of a man are outside his body. The penis is positioned in front of the scrotum. Within the scrotum sac are the testicles. When a young man reaches puberty the testicles begin to produce sperm — the reproductive cells.

During sexual stimulation, the penis fills with blood, and grows hard and erect so that it can slip into the vagina. The sperm then passes from the testicles through the urethra in a milky fluid called semen.

At a time of heightened, emotional excitement, 100 to 300 million sperm are ejected through the urethra into the vagina of a woman. This intensely pleasurable experience is called orgasm. Following the sexual climax is a period of relaxation and usually sleep.[2]

MALE REPRODUCTIVE ORGANS

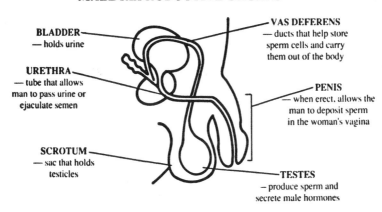

BLADDER — holds urine

URETHRA — tube that allows man to pass urine or ejaculate semen

SCROTUM — sac that holds testicles

VAS DEFERENS — ducts that help store sperm cells and carry them out of the body

PENIS — when erect, allows the man to deposit sperm in the woman's vagina

TESTES — produce sperm and secrete male hormones

Now you can understand — guys are very sex-oriented creatures, but created in the image of God. If a guy understands that this is the way God has put his personality and body together, then he can take action to bring his body and personality under the control of God's Spirit.

HOW DO I RESPOND TO HIM?

Girls, you need to help guys respond the way God wants them to. Remember these suggestions as you try to help the guys you date.

Understand him. A guy faces tremendous sexual pressure. In addition to his strong physical desires, he has emotional needs that cause him to be too aggressive. He wants someone to love him and the only way he knows to express that need is sexually, partially since that aspect of a relationship is so emphasized in our society. He needs to know other ways to develop a love relationship. By helping to keep the physical relationship to a minimum, you can help him know how to express real love.

Not only does a guy have emotional needs, but he

also has a need to prove his masculinity. Why do you think he shows off and does stupid things in front of you? This goes back a long way — "Me caveman, you cavewoman. Me conquer you." He's too sophisticated to drag you by the hair, but he is trying to prove that he's a man. And he needs to. So when you see him demonstrate character — gentleness, hard work, sensitivity, spiritual strength — praise him for these qualities.

And girls, you must understand that most guys are ignorant of the needs of women. Even if a guy understands you, he won't know how to meet your needs on his own. Teach him. Take the time to communicate what your needs are and how he can meet them.

Be patient with him. Girls are generally one to two years ahead of guys in their maturity. You can patiently, positively encourage a guy in his personal growth to

- control his feelings;
- talk through differences without losing his temper;
- accept criticism graciously;
- find constructive outlets for frustration (like exercise);
- build his self-confidence;
- set goals;
- become involved in helping others;
- spend time with friends with the same values;
- get involved in a church that teaches how to follow Jesus;
- seek God with all his heart.

The Bible challenges you to lead your life "with patience, forbearing one another with love" (Ephesians 4:2). That's what every guy needs — your loving patience.

Build respect. Girls, this is your most powerful resource not only to attract the man God has for you, but also to help you handle the sexual aspect of your dating relationships.

What is at stake is your dignity. Dignity is your sense of honor and self-worth that God has given you. You are more than an animal — you are created in the image of God. Relating dignity and sex, Dawson McAllister says:

> Because sex and dignity involve the most personal parts of both our bodies and our inner persons, sex and dignity are linked. Each of us places a heavy value on our physical bodies and our sexual needs. When we misuse our bodies by submitting to our sexual desires, we degrade them and actually tear at our personal worth.[3]

When you give away your respect you will feel that you have been ripped off and something is desperately messed up. When you hold on to it, you not only increase your own honor, but also that of the guy you're dating.

More specifically, guys and girls react to sex in opposite ways. A guy will want to be intimate with you. Some guys want to see how far you will go. But if he really respects you, once you have made your standards clear, he will not pressure you. He may seem ticked off, but inside it pleases him that you are not "easy" like other girls.

But watch out for the *trap*. You have high standards — you haven't let any guy get to first base sexually. But because you care for this one, you permit him to go too far. Then what happens? What you think is pleasing him is actually repelling him. His respect for you goes out the window.

If you respond to him properly, you will "be devoted to one another in brotherly love. [You will] honor one another above yourselves" (Romans 12:10).

Remember, a guy can respect a girl without loving her, but he can never love her without respecting her.

Now that you understand these differences, you can understand at least a little more why guys act the way they do. Don't be intimidated. Rather, take the challenge to learn how guys operate. Stand in awe of the great God who created them and said that they are "fearfully and wonderfully made" (Psalm 139:14).

ACTION SECTION

Understanding

1.   In what three ways do guys act weird? How do you respond to that?

Weird Ways   My Response

(1)—————————   ————————————

(2)—————————   ————————————

(3)—————————   ————————————

Patience

2.   Write down one action you can take to express patience concerning each of those things that are weird.

(1)————————————————————————

(2)————————————————————————

(3)————————————————————————

Respect

3.   What three actions have you taken in the past that have caused you to lose the respect of guys?

(1)————————————————————————

(2)————————————————————————

(3)————————————————————————

4.   What three actions do you need to take to gain respect?

(1)————————————————————————

(2)————————————————————————

(3)————————————————————————

3

Why Are Girls So Strange? ♥

Guys, have you ever asked yourself:
- Why are women so strange?
- Why do girls giggle and talk with each other so much?
- Is there any way to understand females?
- Are all women so emotional?
- Why can't I get a girl to pay attention to me?
- Why can't I get a girl to quit paying attention to me?

Some guys explained it this way: "They expect to be pampered all the time," or "The little things are so important to them — too important," or "They are so influenced by emotions," or "They don't know what they want." One guy summed it up in exasperation, "They're dangerous!"

The same fun experiment that was conducted on the guys that we explained in the last chapter was conducted on the women as well.

The ladies werc wircd with the electrodes on their pulses. The meter was attached. When they were shown a picture of a car, their pulses dropped off. (Most women aren't into cars.) Then they were shown a picture of a flower. Their pulse rates climbed. (Most women love flowers.) Then they saw a picture of a baby. WWOONNGG. Their pulse shot right to the top of the meter. (That's the mothering instinct coming out.) Then, they viewed a picture of a naked man. Flop! The pulse rates often dropped. Most women are wired for love and romance, not just sex.

WHAT ARE GIRLS LIKE?

Women are infinitely different from men. But how?

In Her Spirit

Just as guys have "a God-shaped vacuum," so do girls. They need Jesus Christ. But they respond to that need for God differently. Women are more *tender* — warm and intimate by nature. God made them that way.

But without Jesus Christ their need for love and strength is not met. Therefore, in order to meet that need they look for intimacy in a physical relationship. They often look to sex, because they want protection and security. When women try to get protection and security through their bodies, they destroy themselves.

However, when a women responds to Jesus Christ, she fills the "God-shaped vacuum" and puts herself under the protection and love of the Ultimate Velvet-Covered Brick — Jesus Christ. Then she has love, security and protection. That, in turn, gives her the inner strength to withstand the pressure of a man. She becomes a woman of dignity whom everyone respects. Now isn't that the kind of girl you're looking for?

In Her Personality

In a woman's personality (mind, emotions and will),

love controls her more than sex. Sex is only part of the overall picture of love for a girl. They want to know they are loved before they give themselves sexually. That's because girls respond to their feelings (not to basic desires like guys). To them, to feel secure, loved and romanced is more important than the physical desires. The guy wants to consume the pizza; the girl wants the plates to be clean. The guy wants lots of pepperoni; the girl wants pretty napkins. The guy wants food; the girl wants "atmosphere." When a girl is attracted to a guy she thinks first of *love* — then sex.

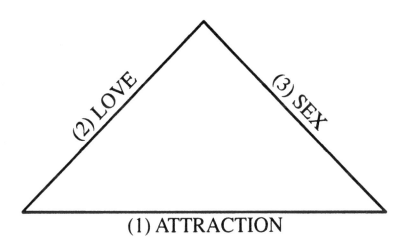

(1) ATTRACTION

Because of their personalities, girls have three characteristics that affect them sexually.

They are romantic. Women are into love and romance. When a girl goes out with a guy, often he is thinking *sex* while *she* is thinking love. Say you're at a movie and you want to hold her physically and make out. She is probably more interested in the love story on the screen: the beauty, the relationship, the romance. While most guys are ready for sex just about any time, any place, most girls are stimulated by tender thoughts, kind deeds, special treatment, flowers, a soft touch.

In fact, according to a recent survey, girls feel strongly romantic about a number of things on dates. In order, they are: fireplaces, stormy skies, candlelight, the seashore, tanned skin, a favorite men's cologne or aftershave, a well-groomed appearance, mountains, the woods, a man dressed up when he is not usually seen that way, slow music, a full moon, a head of well-groomed hair, rustic places and picnics. Big turn-offs for girls are explicit sex scenes and a man's sweaty smell.[1]

Because of this need for romance there is a slower arousal of sexual desire. Most girls do not need sex as a release like guys do; they prefer romantic love before they give themselves sexually.

They are fantasizers. As a result of their desire for romance, girls build castles in their minds, with white knights coming to rescue the damsel in distress. The girl imagines what it would be like to be with you. She dreams of how you would ask her out, and how you would come by her house to take her out for a candlelight dinner. You would both be dressed up, and you would treat her like a queen. You would talk to her tenderly. When the date is over you'd take her hand and kiss her good night at the door. Those kinds of dreams will keep a girl happy a long time.

They want security. When a guy takes advantage of a girl sexually, she starts feeling used. That creates tremendous insecurity. It's difficult for girls to experience loose, casual sexual relationships and still be happy, even if they are the ones pursuing and initiating sex.

A girl needs the confidence that she belongs to someone who also belongs to her. This need for security is so strong that many girls have given themselves in a sexual way, hoping that it would help them get their man. Just the opposite happens.

Only in marriage can a girl find this security. When the guy doesn't take complete responsibility, she can't be sure that he is really committed to her.

When a girl has sex outside of marriage she experiences three harmful effects that relate to her insecurity:

1. Her unfulfilled emotional needs lead to frustration and bitterness.

2. She can develop crippling emotional habits. She keeps looking for long-lasting relationships through sex, but only gets short-term pleasure and long-lasting emotional pain. She can become a slave to her own glands!

3. She experiences deep disappointment resulting from the use of sex to fulfill the need for love.[2]

In marriage, security is built because she knows that her husband is committed to her.

In Her Body

All of these female needs and desires are connected to a body that responds sexually.

The primary sex organs of a woman are inside her body. In the female reproductive system the primary organ is the uterus, or womb. This pear-shaped, hollow muscular organ (about four inches long) is capable of expanding to accommodate a full-size infant. At each side of the uterus is one of the two ovaries which contain the eggs that, when combined with the man's sperm, begin life.

After a girl reaches puberty — between ages ten and fourteen — each month one of these ovaries produces a ripened egg which is released into the fallopian tube connected to the uterus. The release is called ovulation. If there is sexual intercourse during this time, the egg may be fertilized by the sperm. The fertilized egg moves into the uterus, and begins to grow into a human baby. If the egg is not fertilized, it passes out of the body with the blood and mucous lining of the uterus during menstruation. This cycle repeats itself every month.

The cervix, or neck of the uterus, opens into the vagina, a canal of muscle and tissue that leads to the outside of the body. Both the cervix and vagina can expand to accommodate the size of a newborn infant. The entrance to the vagina is partially encircled by a soft flexible membrane called the hymen. (The hymen may be broken during the first act of intercourse or during some other prior physical activity.)

The female reproductive system is protected by the outer covering, the vulva, which is made of two layers of soft fleshy folds. These join at the upper end to form the clitoris, a small extension of flesh that is especially sensitive to sexual stimulation. Beneath the clitoris is the urethra, the opening through which the urine is eliminated. Below the urethra is the opening of the vagina where the act of sexual intercourse takes place.

During sexual intercourse the woman experiences an all-over excitement in which there may or may not be local sensations in her genitals. A woman's response in intercourse develops more slowly to climax and then gradually tapers off. When the man has an orgasm, the millions of sperm make their way through the opening in the cervix, up the uterus, and into the fallopian tube. If an egg is present in the tube and one of the sperm invades it, pregnancy occurs. That is called conception. A baby is alive.[3]

FEMALE REPRODUCTIVE ORGANS

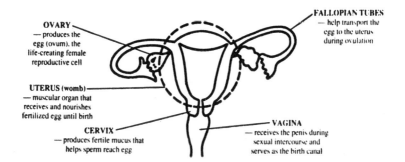

OVARY
— produces the egg (ovum), the life-creating female reproductive cell

FALLOPIAN TUBES
— help transport the egg to the uterus during ovulation

UTERUS (womb)
— muscular organ that receives and nourishes fertilized egg until birth

CERVIX
— produces fertile mucus that helps sperm reach egg

VAGINA
— receives the penis during sexual intercourse and serves as the birth canal

HOW DO I RESPOND TO HER?

Guys, girls want to love you. You need to learn to respond to them the way God wants you to. These suggestions will help you.

Discover her needs. Find out what her needs are — emotionally and spiritually — and do all you can to meet them. For example, she probably has a need for security. Let her know that you can be counted on for support, and encourage her to find her ultimate security in her relationship with the Lord. Tell her often that you appreciate her not only for what she does, but for *who she is* — a woman needs to hear that. For more specifics, read *Dating: Picking (and Being) a Winner.*

Learn to love. Girls have a tremendous need for love. That love expresses itself as

- patient
- kind
- not jealous
- not hurtful
- not arrogant
- not insisting on its own way
- not irritable

- not resentful
- not enjoying wrong, but right
- protective
- trusting
- enduring
- never failing (1 Corinthians 13:4-8)

Only Jesus Christ, through the Holy Spirit, can bring that kind of love. When you desire those qualities in your life, then you will yield to Jesus and learn how to express love that will come across as tenderness and sensitivity. (To learn how to develop each quality better, read our book *Love: Making It Last.*)

Develop maturity. Because they develop more quickly, girls are ahead of you here. You can develop maturity by

- controlling your physical desires (Exercise a lot! See chapter 8);
- passing up immediate pleasure to reach your future goals;
- not being selfish to satisfy your needs;
- putting the other person ahead of you;

- admitting when you are wrong and not blaming others;
- getting involved in a church group that teaches from the Bible clearly about Jesus;
- seeking God with all your heart.

When you focus on these goals, you will "in all things grow up into him who is the Head, that is, Christ" (Ephesians 4:15).

Accept responsibility. In order to be a loving and responsible husband in the future, you need to learn responsibility now. Here are some ways you can do that:

- Obey your parents immediately and without complaining. In fact, do it cheerfully.
- Accept responsibility for chores around your home.
- Be diligent in your school work.
- Work with excellence at your job, if you have one.
- Give 100 percent in all of your extracurricular activities.
- Develop spiritual leadership by taking on a specific role or task in your youth group.
- Set your dating standards and hold to them. (See chapter 12 in *Dating: Picking (and Being) a Winner.)*

Responsibility is a quality that will attract the woman God has for you. It will also help you handle the sexual aspect of your dating relationships.

When you are tempted to get involved sexually, remember that you are responsible for your actions. Outside of marriage it's impossible for you to take on all the responsibility that comes with sexual involvement. You will be frustrated and she will feel used.

G. K. Chesterton explained it like this:

> I loathe the thought of a woman feeling I may have treated her like some sort of spittoon . . . It takes all your energy, patience, and sympathy building anything worthwhile with one woman. But maybe many men are more interested in knocking over rather than building anything solid with a woman. Sex at its best requires that you're there with your

partner totally — body, mind, heart, imagination — that takes
responsible commitment. It's nothing to play with either . . .
you can ruin the whole . . . thing for life, or spend many
years and a hard struggle recapturing its proper use.[4]

Nothing can take the place of responsibility. That
includes not letting a girl push you beyond your limits.
Many girls will call guys up, hint about dates, pass messages
through friends about how attractive a guy is, even make the
move for sex on a date. As a responsible guy, you cannot
respond to these schemes. You have to politely let girls
know you will not give in to their pressure.

A guy can give his time, money, attention and even
his love. But he cannot say honestly that he has taken responsibility until marriage. When the evening is over, he
sends her home to someone else. That someone else buys
the clothes, pays the bills, calls the doctor, stays up with her
all night if she is sick.

If a man is a man, he will be responsible.

Now you know why girls respond to you the way
they do. Don't shy away from them because you don't understand them. Rather, *initiate* relationships with girls so you can
learn how they operate. The great God who created them,
made you. And He will teach you how to understand them
and relate to them.

ACTION SECTION

Understanding

1. In what three ways do girls act strange? How do
you respond to that?

Strange Ways   My Response

(1)_____   _____

(2)_____   _____

(3)_____   _____

Her Needs

2.   Write down a way you can meet the need a girl is expressing in one of the ways she is strange.

_____

_____

Love

3.   Write down one action you can take to express real love to her in response to one of the ways she is strange.

_____

_____

Maturity

4.   What is one action you need to take to develop maturity? Start this week.

_____

_____

Responsibility

5.   What have you done in the past that has shown irresponsibility toward girls?

(1)_____

(2)_____

(3)_____

6.   What actions do you need to take to become responsible?

(1)_____

(2)_____

(3)_____

7.   To protect yourself from sexual irresponsibility, make the following commitment to yourself and your future dates:

I, _____, of my own free will am declaring my intention not to become sexually involved before marriage because I cannot take full responsibility for the other person in case of pregnancy or any other ill effect, whether physical, emotional or spiritual.

Signed _____

Dated _____

4

Why Wait For Sex? ♥

*I*f two people really care for each other, why is it wrong for them to make love?"

We have been asked that question hundreds of times. It's a good question — with a good answer.

If your parents want a well-groomed yard with as few weeds as possible, they have to work hard. But after a long day's work, when they look out on the lawn, you hear them comment, "Doesn't the yard look beautiful?" And it does, because the sod is cared for and in its proper place.

But if you dig up a hunk of that sod with a shovel, take it in the house and put it on your mom's rug, what will she say? "Get that dirt out of here!" Why would she say that? Just a few minutes ago she said it was beautiful. Is it beautiful sod or nasty dirt? That depends on what you do with it. In the yard, it's beautiful. On the rug, it's dirt.

That's similar to the way you handle your sexuality.

If you use it in marriage, like God designed it, then it's beautiful. If you use it outside of marriage and outside of God's plan, then it becomes dirty: sick sex.

You have a choice. You can give your body away before marriage, and sex will be dirty. Or you can wait to give your body to that one special person in marriage, and sex will be beautiful. You can choose. God's way. Or your way.

CHOOSING YOUR WAY

When you choose your way, you'll get sexual "thrills and chills." You'll enjoy a certain excitement that comes from a girl seducing you or a guy romancing you. One man described it this way:

> She put her arms around him and kissed him, and with a saucy look she said, "I've decided to forget our quarrel! I was just coming to look for you and here you are! My bed is spread with lovely colored sheets of finest linen imported from Egypt, perfumed with myrrh, aloes, and cinnamon. Come on, let's take our fill of love until morning, for my husband is away on a long trip. He has taken a wallet full of money with him, and won't return for several days."

That's from the Bible — Proverbs 7:13-21 (TLB). See, God really does know what life is like.

But you have to know that if you have sex before marriage, you can experience many devastating effects. Here are some of the most obvious ones that wipe you out immediately:

1. Loss of virginity
2. Guilt and fear
3. Bad memories and flashbacks
4. Sexually transmitted diseases
5. Unwanted pregnancy
6. Illegitimate child
7. Forced marriage
8. Hurt parents
9. Self-hatred

10. Spiritual bondage
11. Possible abortion

The writer of Proverbs describes the devastation of not waiting:

> He followed her as an ox going to the butcher, or as a stag that is trapped, waiting to be killed with an arrow through its heart. He was as a bird flying into a snare, not knowing the fate awaiting it there. Listen to me, young men, and not only listen but obey; don't let your desires get out of hand; don't let yourself think about her. Don't go near her; stay away from where she walks, lest she tempt you and seduce you. For she has been the ruin of multitudes — a vast host of men have been her victims (Proverbs 7:22-26, TLB).

CHOOSING GOD'S WAY

God wants you to "do it" His way. In 1 Thessalonians 4:3 the Bible says, "It is God's will that you should be holy; that you should avoid sexual immorality."

Why doesn't God leave you a loophole to express your desires freely? Because He knows how you operate best. When you are dealing with a complex machine like your body, you don't always understand how it works. When the designer of your car says to keep gas and oil in it, keep the tires pumped up with air and get it tuned up every 15,000 miles, you do it, even though you may not understand why. God says WAIT. You have the Designer's word for it — that's the best way.

In fact, when two people love each other in marriage, sex will be much more than "thrills and chills." When you get caught up in the embrace of God's love that He will give to you and your partner, your love — including sex — will be the very best for you. That's what God wants. That's His will for you. And that's worth waiting for!

Already you can see waiting is not negative, but positive. God has your best interests at heart. His desire is to protect you and to provide for you. And to show you how much He wants the best for you, He has given you some positive reasons to wait.

REASONS TO WAIT

Protect the Gift of Your Virginity

Do you care if your husband or wife has sex before you get married? Sure you do! If you have waited, you want to marry someone who has waited also.

So you intend to wait and to marry someone who has waited. You might explain it like this: "I think marriage is the right place for sex, and I want my partner and me to wait." But it's not that easy when your hormones start hopping, the juices start pumping and the desire to be close to someone of the opposite sex becomes almost unbearable. The plan to wait gets lost in the heat of the moment. You begin to think, "What's the big deal? Let's do it now."

So what is the big deal about being a virgin? All of the input around you — friends, TV, music, etc. — tells you that sexual intercourse is only a normal bodily function for you to enjoy and that losing your virginity is a test of how mature you are. That's a lie! The truth is that the more inexperienced and innocent you are when you marry, the greater your sexual satisfaction with your husband or wife will be.

That's what the Bible means in 1 Thessalonians 4:4 when it says that "each one of you know how to take a wife for himself in holiness and in honor." "Holy" means "set apart for God's purposes," and "honor" means you are very special. You can say your virginity is the sign that you are set apart and very special in God's eyes.

As you wait to enter marriage, your virginity will result in several important benefits:

The white gown is not a farce. As a bride you can walk down the aisle and as a groom you can wait to receive her, knowing that you are pure before God and before each other.

Pregnancy is no problem. When two people refrain from sexual intercourse before marriage, obviously pregnancy is not an issue.

Birth control is not 100 percent effective. Birth control supposedly lets you have sex without the danger of pregnancy. Many say the big solution to the teen pregnancy problem is "safer sex." Society says, "Be careful — use birth control." But with more than one out of every ten teenage girls getting pregnant each year, somebody obviously hasn't explained too well how birth control works.

In fact, most students never use birth control. They think like this: "Only bad people have sex. Therefore, if I use birth control, I'm planning to be bad. Instead, I'll just let it happen like it does in the movies." In their mind, if they have sex in a moment of passion, it's OK. As a result of this thinking, only one in three sexually active students uses birth control, and most of them had been having sex an average of twelve months before they began to use contraceptives.[1]

There are all kinds of weird ideas about birth control.
• "I can't get pregnant the first time I have sex."
• "I am safe if I have sex standing up."
• "I won't get pregnant if I douche afterwards."
• "I'll take the pill just before I have sex, and I won't get pregnant."

The only 100-percent guaranteed birth control method for the person who is not married is virginity. That means abstaining from sexual intercourse.

The issue is not birth control, but *virginity*.

Unless you've lived through an unplanned pregnancy with someone, it's difficult to understand the devastation. The girl is heartsick and the guy is confused, scared and angry. Both are hurt and disappointed. More important than all of that, a third, innocent victim — the baby — has to live, or die, with the consequences of their passion.

When you wait you avoid all of that hurt.

Trust in each other is complete. Sex before marriage creates tremendous insecurity on the part of the girl and a lack of respect for the girl on the part of the guy. Those feelings cast doubt on the relationship and its future. If the couple does get married, the question will eventually arise: If he (or she) had sex before marriage, will he do it after marriage, too? All of that adds up to destroyed trust. When you wait, you can fully trust one another.

Sexual diseases are not a worry. Sexually transmitted diseases are rampant. New types and strains are being discovered all the time. Most don't respond to medication. They are miserable at best. They bring death at worst. That is a high price to pay for a few minutes of pleasure. The way to insure against disease is to wait.

No guilt feelings from bad memories. One girl wrote: "I was madly in love with this guy. One night when we were driving around in the car, he suddenly stopped and told me that if I ever wanted to see him again I would have sex with him right now. I loved him so much and I didn't want to lose him, so I did it. I hate myself and him." What was once a special relationship is now a bad dream. Filled with guilt, one student said, "God, I feel dirty." When you wait, you will never have to worry about spoiling a present or future relationship with guilt or bad memories.

Conversations with your kids about sex can be done with a clear conscience. When students can't resist sexual temptation, we ask them, "Do you know if your parents struggled with this?" Often they say angrily, "I know my parents had sex before marriage. That's how I got here." You don't want to begin, or continue, a cycle that will negatively affect your children. Your behavior now will affect your children's attitudes toward sex later. Barry says, "Recently I talked to my son about the facts of life. Because I had kept myself pure, our conversation was a blast!" By remaining a virgin until marriage you will be able to look them in the eye and tell your kids that the way you waited is the way they need to wait.

Learning sex together in marriage is fun. Anyone can have sex. But what you want is the best sex, and that takes practice. In marriage you have the freedom to practice and to talk about your sex life, to say what you like and what you don't. That makes for better sex. Sex is an art. Waiting to learn that skill together in marriage is fun.

Your virginity is a precious gift God has given to

you. If you lose it, you lose something of great value. When you wait until marriage to have sex, your virginity isn't lost; it's transformed into the experience of total dynamic oneness!

Someday you're going to get married. You will love that person more than anyone else. When you close the door to your room behind you on your wedding night, what will you say? "I've had sex with Bob, Jim, Mark and Andy (or Susan, Ann, Michelle and Sharon). Everybody else has used me. Here's what's left."

How much better to close the door and say, "Here is my body. I present it to you, clean and pure. Nobody else has touched it. It's an unopened gift for you to open now. It's all yours. I give it with love."

Learn How to Love, Not Lust

We've heard many young people say, "I'm in love. I know it. It's the real thing. We can't stand to be apart. I'm sure it's going to last forever."

What hurts is to talk with that same person two months later and hear this: "I was just sure it was right. We were so much in love. It started out great, but then we got physically involved."

That's what happens when you get into "the passion of lust" that 1 Thessalonians 4:5 talks about: "not in passionate lust like the heathen, who do not know God."

As long as your relationships are based on lust you will never wait to have sex. When they are based on love you will want to wait until marriage for sex. When you get involved in a relationship, how do you know if it's love or lust?

LUST	LOVE
• Lust is based on selfishness. ("I want what I want when I want it.")	• Love is based on putting the other person's needs first.
• Lust gives in to hormones (physical desires).	• Love operates with self-control.

- Lust wants only physical satisfaction.

- Love cares about the social, mental, emotional and spiritual areas of a person's life as well as the physical.

- Lust either gets irritated or pouts if it doesn't get satisfaction.

- Love is patient.

- Lust is jealous of any competition.

- Love is kind to everyone.

- Lust goes for instant gratification.

- Love takes time to grow.

- Lust doesn't require partners to share openly.

- Love communicates freely.

- Lust is an instinct.

- Love is a commitment that comes as a result of the Holy Spirit working in your life.

- Lust walks away after it is satisfied.

- Love hangs in there over the long haul.

- Lust says "I loved it."

- Love says "I love you."

What do you want to build your relationships on — lust or love? If lust is the answer, you'll never know how to have a healthy relationship with the opposite sex. If the answer is love, then you'll know how to build healthy relationships now and a healthy marriage later. Now that's worth waiting for!

Build Healthy Relationships

You have watched couples like this (or maybe you've been one): This week they say, "I love him. I am so happy."

"She's the neatest girl I've ever met."

"He's the greatest. We're in love."

Two weeks later they're saying, "You creep, I hate you."

"I never want to see you again."

"You want your jacket back? OK, here it is — with the sleeves cut off!"

"You want your picture? Here it is, torn into a thousand pieces!"

What is happening here? Obviously these two people don't know how to have a healthy relationship. In 1 Thessalonians 4:6, Paul explains that a relationship built on sex outside of marriage is not healthy because "no one should wrong his brother, or take advantage of him." When a relationship gets too physical, one person in the relationship (or both) is taking advantage of the other. You try to start over, but every time, the physical gets too heavy. It hurts both you and the other person. Why does it happen again and again? Because you are taking advantage of each other. You don't know how to build a healthy relationship. You can't beat the break-up habit because you've put too much emphasis on sex. You have lost sight of what God is trying to do in your life and in the life of the other person.

Your relationship with God. When sex controls you, your relationship with God goes into neutral. He seems to be a million miles away. You feel like your prayers don't reach the ceiling. You even begin to doubt if God exists.

Your relationship with each other. When you have sex outside of marriage, you want to be intimate and close. You want sex to bind you together. Instead, it *tears you apart.* What started out as a tender expression now produces tension. Your relationship suffers in several areas:

• Breakdown in communication. Now instead of long talks, you are looking for ways to be alone to make love. Without talking, your relationship is crippled. More sex only puts a Band-Aid on a broken bone that will never correctly heal.[2]

• Shallow relationship. Sex is the easiest and most direct route to intimacy, but it is not the best. Why? The glue of sex is not strong enough to hold the relationship together. The qualities that make a relationship hold together — trust, honesty, openness, deep friendship and spiritual depth — take time and effort to develop. A heavy-duty emphasis on sex causes the relationship to come unglued.[3]

• Guilt. Sex before marriagc causes you to feel guilty. Why? Because you are. This guilt prevents you from building the relationship.

• Insecurity and loss of respect. In real love there is no one else. But premarital sex knocks the props out from under the security a girl needs and the respect a guy needs.

"If he made love to me, I wonder if there are others."

"All he ever wants is sex."

"I just don't respect her anymore."

When you don't wait, security and respect are lost.

• Comparison to others. If you have sex before marriage, when you get married you will flash back. You will think, "That guy kisses better than my husband." "She makes love better than my wife." Or if your sexual experience is bad before marriage, all the fear and anger of the past will cause you to freeze emotionally. As a result, you are not completely free to love your marriage partner.

Your relationship with your future mate. How will having sex now affect your future marriage and mate? Research by sociologist and author Roy Short shows that:

- Men prefer to marry women who have not had sexual intercourse with someone else.
- The marriage will more likely end in divorce.
- Extramarital affairs will more likely occur.
- Women who have had premarital sex are twice as likely to have extramarital affairs than those who have not.
- Premarital sex may cause you to marry a person not right for you — sex can blind you.[4]

Your relationship with yourself. When you have sex, a part of your personality stays with that other person forever. Like an apple sliced with a knife and given out to several different people, every time you have sex with a different person, your personality is being divided and handed out. You can never recover it.

Because sex is so powerful, it creates strong emotional bonds between partners. These bonds can make you feel that the relationship is deeper than it really is — thinking you know your partner and your partner knows you better than you actually do. You become emotionally "sliced":

- You have unfulfilled needs that cause you to get frustrated and bitter.
- You hang on to the relationship, not out of love, but out of fear and insecurity.
- You wanted intimacy and love but are disappointed that all you got was sex.

If you wait, you will learn to build healthy relationships. And God's promise in 1 Thessalonians 4:9 will be true for you: "You yourselves have been taught by God to love each other."

Now that kind of healthy relationship is worth waiting for!

Have the Best Marriage

Sex outside of marriage isn't bad because it's "naughty." It's bad because it gets in the way of something better.[5] God is not against your enjoying sex. Not at all. But He wants you to enjoy it to the ultimate. That's why 1 Thessalonians 4:4 says "to keep clear of all sexual sin so that each of you will marry in holiness and honor" (TLB). Men, that means that you have the knowledge and skill to possess a woman sexually[6] and that you are willing to pay a high price for her because of her value.[7]

It's not that sex wouldn't feel good now. It probably would. And at the time it may make you feel close to that person. But God wants you to have a far deeper and more thrilling closeness: total dynamic oneness in marriage.

What you have seen of marriage may not be all that hot. "Who needs it?" you say. Many of those not-so-hot marriages got messed up because the couple did not wait until marriage for sex. Sorry marriage is not what God designed. He designed it to be enjoyed to the max. Sex is meant for that kind of marriage. God's desire is for you to

have the best marriage.
- He wants you to spend a lifetime in love with your husband or wife.
- He wants to see you grow more in love with each passing year.
- He wants you to live without the fear of divorce.
- He wants you to live in complete trust of each other.

That's what marriage means for followers of Jesus Christ. With that kind of love, sex is the natural, beautiful expression of commitment.[8]

Barry illustrates this: "My son has a guitar. The problem is, all but one string is broken. So when he plays it, all that comes out is a monotone 'twang.' But if he would put all the strings in place, tighten them and tune the guitar, he could play sweet music.

"When God says 'Wait until marriage,' He wants your sex life to be like those guitar strings — not hanging loose, where you'll think you're free to do anything you want with your body, but tightly strung and in tune. Then, at the proper place and time, and with the proper person, you can make 'sweet music' — and not just in your sex life, but in every aspect of your relationship."

Now that's worth waiting for!

LEARN TO SAY NO

Any one of these reasons should be enough to convince you to wait. But, when your hormones get hot, it's not easy. However, you can do it! Titus 2:11,12 tells you why you can: "For the grace of God that brings salvation has appeared to all men. It teaches us to say 'No' to ungodliness and worldly passions, and to live self-controlled, upright and godly lives in this present age." One fantastic solution to help you wait comes leaping out of those verses: Say NO.

You say, "I want to, but it's so hard." Maybe one of these thoughts is yours.

- "I don't want to hurt his feelings."

- "I don't want to lose her approval and love."
- "I am afraid he won't like me."
- "It means a lot to him."
- "I don't want to seem like a tease."
- "I am afraid she will think I don't like her."
- "I want to prove I'm a man."
- "There's nothing else to do."[9]

Right now practice saying no. Go ahead. NO. Say it to yourself. NO. Now say it out loud. NO. That's not so hard. Now call a friend and practice it.

Making the following decisions will help you say no.

Decide to please God. If you say no, some people won't want to go out with you. You must decide to be a God pleaser, not a man pleaser. The apostle Paul asks a good question: "Am I now trying to win the approval of men, or of God? Or am I trying to please men? If I were still trying to please men, I would not be a servant of Christ" (Galatians 1:10).

Decide to say no when it's easy. If you say no in the smaller decisions, you won't have to say no under heavy pressure. Make these decisions now.

- I will not come on as a flirt, tease or easy make.
- I will not go to the "passion pit."
- I will not see X- or R-rated films.
- I will not stay alone at my parents' house (or any other house) with someone of the opposite sex.
- I will not wear "sexy" clothes (unbuttoned too far or fitted too tight).
- I will not let my clothes get unzipped, unbuttoned or unsnapped.
- I will not date a non-Christian.

The Bible encourages these "no" decisions when it says, "Be very careful, then, how you live — not as unwise but as wise" (Ephesians 5:15).

Decide to change if you have already blown it. If you have given in to the pressure in the past, you can start over. Jesus Christ wants you to confess your sin to Him, and

He wants to give you a fresh, new start. "If we confess our sins, he is faithful and just and will forgive us our sins and purify us from all unrighteousness" (1 John 1:9). (See chapter 11 for a more in-depth look.)

Decide to say yes about Jesus Christ. Instead of just saying "No, my mom doesn't want me to," or "No, I'm too tired," say, "No, I can't do that because I am following Jesus Christ." The apostle Paul said, "I am not ashamed of the gospel" (Romans 1:16). When you are not ashamed of Jesus, then He will strengthen you and use you. That will make an impact not only on your date, but also on many others in your school.

Barry remembers someone who had an impact like that on him:

"On my first day at a camp in North Carolina when I was nineteen, I saw a beautiful girl. I took her out.

"After our date, we went down this long, lonely, dark road. Then I tried to kiss her. She said, 'No.' 'Why not?' I asked. I'll never forget her answer. She said, 'Because of Jesus Christ.'

"I remember scratching my head in the dark, thinking *What does Jesus have to do with kissing?* I had never had a girl tell me that before. You know what I did? Instead of dropping her, I wanted to go out with that girl again. I was intrigued by her. My respect for her grew. I never tried to make the move on her again.

"As we talked she told me how to have a personal relationship with Jesus Christ. The reason I'm a follower of Jesus today is because one girl had enough guts to say 'No...because of Jesus Christ.'"

You can too!

Now that you have decided to wait for sex until marriage, you are probably wondering: "What do I do in the meantime?" We've written a whole book to help you — *Dating: Picking (and Being) a Winner.* You can order it from Reach Out Ministries or your local Christian bookstore.

If you have already blown it, there is hope. Read chapters 11 and 12 in this book.

ACTION SECTION

1. Between now and the time you marry, you will be tempted not to wait. From what you have discovered in this chapter, why do you think it is best for you to wait? Give at least three reasons to wait and include a passage from the Bible to go with each.

(1)_____

verse: _____

(2)_____

verse: _____

(3)_____

verse: _____

2. Now fill out the commitment card below. Write your answers from your heart and your convictions about your sex life.

I, _____ , have decided to wait to have sex until I am married because

(1) _____

(2) _____

(3) _____

3. List some of the positive and negative things that might happen to you if you say no to your date:

Positive	Negative
_____	_____
_____	_____
_____	_____
_____	_____
_____	_____
_____	_____

5

How Far Is Too Far? ♥

*S*ex is a progression. Each physical move you make takes you closer to intercourse.

Remember, guys, the first time you went out with your special girl — just the two of you? You spent the entire afternoon getting ready. You took three showers (one in aftershave). You worked for an hour to shave off your one whisker. Then you stood for another hour in front of the mirror squeezing your zits. (There's nothing worse than blackheads and whiteheads to gross out your date.) Why do you take all of this time to get ready? Because you know that going out with this girl is going to be FUN!

Remember, gals, the first time you went out with your special guy — just the two of you? You went on a three-day shopping spree to buy just the right clothes. You fixed your hair fourteen different ways before you got it right. You put on your make-up five times and made eight phone calls to your girl friend to see if you were wearing the right blue earrings. Why? Because you know that going out with this guy is going to be FUN!

And it is! You go out to eat, then to the movies. Once your eyes get adjusted to the dark theater, guys, you see her hand just hanging around on her arm. Her hand is beautiful — long, luscious fingers, with the nails bright red. And the smell! What is that great stuff she's wearing? As it continues to hang around there it appears to have a sign on it: "Please take." Finally, with all of your courage, you grab that beautiful, luscious, sweet-smelling hand with your cold, sweaty, clammy paw. Your pulse rate is now past 150 and climbing. Could anything be more wonderful than this?

On your next date you hold hands, and rub arms. That's standard stuff. But now, during the most boring part of the movie, you do the old "yawn trick" — you stretch as if you are bored, then your arm comes down around her shoulder. Now you are hugging her as she gently cradles her head in your neck. You try to keep from shaking with excitement, but you know that any minute your whole body is going to explode.

Can this last forever? Why can't time stand still? Could life get any better than this?

But both of you want more. What you did a little of last week will be better if you do a little more of it this week. So you go further.

CLOSER AND CLOSER

One move leads to another — drawing you closer and closer to intercourse.

Where do you stop?

Your body says, "Don't ever stop."

Your emotions say, "Right on."

But your conscience says, "Whoa."

How far is too far?

You are cruising down the road in your brand new sports car (dream on). You have your learner's permit, but not your license. You started the car (no problem). You really don't know what you're doing, but the car is on the road and moving (still no problem). Now you want to test the car out, push it to the limit, so you jam the pedal to the floor (problem). Suddenly the car is out of control (big problem). In a moment you will hit a tree, a telephone pole and a fire hydrant (real big problem). Sexually speaking, that's what happens as you move down the road toward sexual intercourse.

The Bible shows how things get out of control. Read 1 Thessalonians 4:3-6:

> It is God's will that you should be holy; that you should avoid sexual immorality, that each of you should learn to control his own body in a way that is holy and honorable, not in passionate lust like the heathen, who do not know God; and that in this matter no one should wrong his brother or take advantage of him. The Lord will punish men for all such sins, as we have already told you and warned you.

Notice that the problem is "sexual immorality" — messing around with sex.

And when you do that, you "wrong" the other person (verse 6). *Guys*, that word means to go beyond the limits, to go further than God wants you to go. When you do that, you "defraud" yourself and your date (verse 6). *Gals*, that word means to rob, to take what doesn't belong to you so that you spoil your future.

One student expressed it this way:

> I've always been a good student. For a long time I didn't date so I could study. But the guys who were dating told me a lot of things, and so I decided to study less and play more. Then I met Michelle. From our first date we liked each other a lot. Then the relationship got more and more physical until we had sex. Both of us were really enjoying ourselves.
>
> One day I woke up and realized how far behind I was in my studies. So I got into the books and quit seeing Michelle for a while. That hurt her and made her angry. Right in the middle of exams she called to tell me she was pregnant.

All I could think of was *How do I get out of this mess?* I was scared. It turned out to be a false alarm. We went through hell for three weeks. Our relationship was finished. I realized that I didn't love her. I felt guilty. She was deeply hurt. We wiped each other out, just for the "fun" of sex.

In messing around with sex this couple went too far and robbed each other of what could have been a wonderful relationship. They drove the car out of control. How did they do that? How could that happen to you?

THOUGHTS (thinking that sexual pleasure satisfies)	ACTIONS (receiving only temporary pleasure)	HABITS (yielding to the sexual desire more and more)

STRONGER ACTIONS (getting the excitement level higher)	STRONGER HABITS (going further to reach the the excitement level)	DISAPPOINT-MENT (desiring but never finding satisfaction)

Once your sexual desires get out of control, you hit those trees, fire hydrants and telephone poles.

PASSION OF LUST	SENSUALITY	DECEPTION	SEXUAL IMMORAL-ITY
(verse 5) letting your thought life and habits get out of control	(verse 6) ("transgress") planning to satisfy the out-of-control sexual desire	(verse 6) ("defraud") arousing sexual desires in another that cannot be fulfilled God's way	(verse 3) having sexual intercourse between two unmarried people

WHERE TO STOP

Having your sexuality out of control is not good in God's eyes. So how do you know how far to go?

Suppose you are driving your car on a dangerous road. The shoulder of the road is narrow and the drop-off very steep — about 200 feet straight down. If you are just seeking a thrill, you will drive as close to the edge of the road as possible to see how close you can get without going over. You say, "Gee, this is fun. I love my car, and it sure does feel good driving it right at the edge. What a view, I can see all the way to the bottom of the mountain. It's exciting to live dangerously." But it never occurs to you what will happen if you slip up and drive one inch closer to the edge. WHOOSH. You are *history*. Dead meat. A goner. Now we have to dig you out of the wreck. Not too smart, right?

But that's the approach most people take with their sex life. "How close to the edge can I get? How far can I go without ruining my life and the life of the person I'm dating? How much fun can I have before I get caught?" That's suicidal. You're asking for it.

Now if you are intelligent, you will drive along that dangerous highway hugging the center line, staying as far away from the edge as you possibly can. You say, "I really do love my car and I love myself, so I want to protect them both."

Hopefully, by now you have decided to take the part of the road that will protect you, your date, your future and the future of your date. If so, these driving instructions will keep you not only from crashing and burning, but also keep you on the road to ultimate sexual satisfaction. They will help you know how far is too far.

Intercourse Is Out

"Is it OK to have sexual intercourse before I get married?"

The answer to that is very clear in 1 Thessalonians 4:3: "Abstain from immorality." That means that God does not want you to have sexual intercourse before you are married. Period.

To "go all the way" before marriage is totally opposed to God's plan for your life. You can see that expressed by Him in many verses in the Bible:

• "Instead we should write to them, telling them to abstain from food polluted by idols, from sexual immorality, from the meat of strangled animals and from blood" (Acts 15:20).

• "'Food for the stomach and the stomach for food'— but God will destroy them both. The body is not meant for sexual immorality, but for the Lord, and the Lord for the body" (1 Corinthians 6:13).

• "Flee from sexual immorality. All other sins a man commits are outside his body, but he who sins sexually sins against his own body. Do you not know that your body is a temple of the Holy Spirit, who is in you, whom you have received from God? You are not your own; you were bought at a price. Therefore honor God with your body" (1 Corinthians 6:18-20).

• "Marriage should be honored by all, and the marriage bed kept pure, for God will judge the adulterer and all the sexually immoral" (Hebrews 13:4).

God's plan for your sex life is that you express it *only* in marriage.

Sex is like a fire. The same fire that warms a house can burn it down. If you take a flaming log out of your fireplace and put it on your mom's rug, you'll not only tick off your mom, but you'll also burn down your house. A fire in the fireplace gives warmth and comfort. A fire outside the limits of the fireplace destroys. The proper place for sex to burn is in the fireplace of the marriage relationship, where it brings warmth to the relationship. Outside of the marriage relationship, sex destroys.[1]

Petting Is Out

"I know sexual intercourse is wrong, but is there anything wrong with petting? It feels so good and it draws us so close that it seems like the right thing to do."

You're right! It does feel good and it does make you feel close. But God tells us that if you do it, it is like hugging one of those burning logs. First Thessalonians 4:4,5 says, "Each one of you should learn to control his own body in a way that is holy and honorable, not in passionate lust like the heathen who do not know God."

In order to understand why God says this, let's define some terms.

Necking: Touching each other from the neck up.
Petting: Touching each other from the neck down.
Petting has many different expressions:

• Hugging so that your hands caress your partner's back and sides.

- Touching breasts and groin through or under cloth-
  ing.
- Lying down together or on top of each other.
- Touching sexual organs in order to reach orgasm.[2]

The above actions feel good, express intimacy and
don't lead to pregnancy. However, is it just intercourse that
leads you through the guardrails and over the edge to crash
and burn at the bottom of the cliff? Should a couple get
involved in those actions which are preliminaries to intercourse if they stop before sexual intercourse?

No way! *Petting is designed by God to end in intercourse.* So, when you put yourself in a position to arouse the
"passionate lust," you have gone too far. Returning to the
fire illustration: Touches light the fire, caresses fuel the flame
and heated passion grows into a mighty blaze.[3] Once you
start petting, your motor gets revved up and it doesn't want
to turn off. In fact, what you want to do is "put the pedal to
the metal" and go all the way. So STOP!

But you say, "We're going to pet, but no more."
That sounds good, but once your body gets going, you lose
the ability to make rational decisions. All those things you
have said about waiting go out the window. Your emotions
and physical desires take over. Then you're headed for big
trouble.

There's another side. Once you begin petting, those
exciting feelings start, and they build. There is steam all
over the windows of the car. The adrenalin is flowing. One
of you decides in this hot and heavy situation that you have
gone too far. Then STOP! BAM. Your body goes berserk.
Your emotions say, "Good grief, what are you doing to me?
You got my motor revved up and now you turn off the en-
gine." *That is frustrating.* You have started something that
you can't finish.

Imagine driving a car along the highway at 55 miles
per hour and throwing the gear into park. You'd kill that
car. It can't stop that fast. It's even worse trying to throw it
into reverse. It's got to keep going—and so do your sexual
motors once they're running.

Over and over we've observed several things about couples who were into petting, and their relationships have one of two endings (and sometimes both):
1. They go all the way.
2. They break up angry, frustrated and deeply hurt.

Going Beyond the Other Person's Limits Is Out

"How can something so beautiful, that makes two people feel so close, not be good?"

That's a good question, but here's the problem: God's guidelines say that "in this matter no one should wrong his brother or take advantage of him" (1 Thessalonians 4:6). In other words, don't go beyond the other person's limits. When you do that, instead of drawing you together, it will drive you apart.

- *Suspicion* sets in — "Am I the only one he/she has ever done this with?"
- *Guilt* weighs heavy — "I love him/her, but I know this is wrong."
- *Fear* overcomes you — "What if he/she breaks up with me?"
- *Communication* breaks down — "All we ever do is make out. We don't talk to each other anymore."
- *Respect* is lost not only for the other person, but also for yourself — "Because she lets me do these things, she must not have many moral values." Or "He's a sex maniac. That's all he ever cares about and I hate it."

Remember, the person you date today will be somebody else's mate tomorrow.[4] Do you want to marry a person who has been involved sexually with someone else? No way, right? Most other people don't either! So you need to keep your hands off in order not to hurt another person's future relationships. If you really care for (and love) someone you are dating, you will never take advantage of that person by going beyond his/her limits.

Intensive Kissing Is Out

"Kissing is so innocent. It's not even below the neck. You gotta be kidding if you think I can date and not even kiss."

You've got to keep going back to what God says. First Thessalonians 4:7 says, "For God did not call us to be impure but to live a holy life." Anything that creates impure thoughts and moves you in rapid progression down the road to sexual intercourse is wrong. Intense kissing heads you down that road. When you get involved in one of those vacuum-cleaner kisses (sucking on each other's lips), is that all you want to do, or do you want more?

We're not trying to figure out how to justify your behavior in order to make it acceptable to you. We're trying to find out how God wants you to respond. The Bible says, "But among you there must not be *even a hint* of sexual immorality or of any kind of impurity" (Ephesians 5:3).

Intense kissing poses practical problems:

It leads to other things. When the motor gets started and the car moves forward, it's difficult to put it in reverse. Your body is designed so that when it reaches one stage it naturally wants to go on to the next stage. Many couples say, "We can't stop." And the further you go, the harder it is to stop.

It intensifies the relationship. Your feelings for each other are heightened and the physical attraction is strong; therefore, your relationship seems to be more serious than it really is. You think it's love, when really it's infatuation. Enjoying the way the other person kisses is not a solid basis for a relationship.

It lies to the other person. Your body says that you care deeply for the other person. If you care so deeply, why is it that you're kissing someone different every month? What you're saying with your body is not necessarily what you really mean with your heart.

It stifles your relationship. When the physical becomes the most important aspect of your relationship — and intense kissing starts you on that road — then making-out takes the place of communication. The relationship stops growing. Guys especially get their minds preoccupied, not with talking but with making-out. It may be more physically pleasurable to kiss than to talk, but you clobber the relationship.

You are probably asking, "So what *can* I do?" We're not writing this to tell you, "Thou shalt not kiss more than 4.2 seconds." All of this is not a bunch of thou-shalt-not rules to keep you miserable while everybody else is having fun. Remember, God's purpose is not to keep you from having fun, but to *protect* you.

So where does a nice kiss fit in? Well, there are all kinds of kisses:

- a good night kiss
- a good morning kiss (only after brushing to avoid morning mouth)
- a kiss from your sister (booooring)
- a dry kiss (when you have a cold and your lips are cracked)
- a juicy kiss (when you have a runny nose)
- a vacuum-cleaner kiss (sucking on the lips)
- a dishwasher kiss (spit flies everywhere)
- a metallic kiss (the worst: your braces get locked)

A kiss can be a peck on the cheek, or one of those half-hour deals where you come out with your lips raw and bleeding.

How do you determine whether or not to kiss? And how to kiss?

1. Determine what a kiss means to you.

2. Realize that a kiss starts physical contact.

3. Let a kiss reveal your heart, not your hormones.

First Thessalonians 5:26 says, "Greet all the brothers with a holy kiss." Remember, God is not against a good kiss — He just wants it holy!

Overstepping Your Limits Is Out

"What difference does it make if I go a little beyond what I've said I would do? I'm growing up. I'm maturing. I can handle it."

You are maturing physically, emotionally and spiritually. That's great! You want to keep on maturing, too, so don't slow down your progress. Sexually driving yourself over the cliff will definitely hamper your progress. Wrecks always delay your getting to your destination. You will wreck when you go beyond what your conscience tells you.

As followers of Jesus, we have the Holy Spirit living inside of us. One role the Holy Spirit plays is to convince you of anything you are doing that is wrong — no matter how large or small it is. If you have set certain standards (and you will before you finish this book), and if you violate those standards and get physically involved anyway, the Bible says that is sin (Romans 14:14). Even if it's as innocent as a kiss, if God has shown you not to do it, then it is wrong.

The exciting thing is that the Holy Spirit will show you when you are wrong. He will speak to your conscience. He will cause you to feel guilty. "Exciting?" you say. "Feeling guilty is exciting?" Yes, because you will know where your limits are. You will know when you are outside those limits and you will take steps to get back. You will know that when you are inside your limits, God will be pleased with your behavior.

Respond to the Holy Spirit's conviction by asking forgiveness and getting back on the road. If you don't, you will become calloused. The Holy Spirit will continue to speak to you, but you won't be able to hear.

One way to test yourself is to ask: "Do I have the same moral convictions that I had six months ago?" If you've gone beyond your limits, go to God and confess. Ask Him to reset your limits, to make you sensitive to the Holy Spirit and to give you the strength to follow Him.[5]

If you follow these principles in determining how far you go, you'll be very close to God's design which will protect you from going over the cliff or hitting a tree. And He will keep you on the road to His wonderful plan for your sex life.

DECIDE YOUR LIMITS

You're probably asking, "I have all of these sexual desires — what can I do?"

You can use these guidelines to set your own sexual limits.

Let God's Spirit Take Control

"These desires inside of me feel like they will explode!"

We understand. The only way to handle that is to give your sexual thoughts and feelings to God every day. Ask the Holy Spirit to control your desires. Jesus said, "Apart from me you can do nothing" (John 15:5). That's especially true in this area of your life. You've probably tried to set sexual limits before, and you've blown it, so you know you can't do it yourself.

Let the Lord take control. First Thessalonians 4:8 tells you that God "gives you His Holy Spirit" so you can have the strength to follow His design for your sexuality. If you mess up, confess immediately to the Lord and turn the control over to Him again. There's a verse in the Bible that's great to know when you struggle with this area: "I can do all things through Christ who strengthens me" (see Philippians 4:13). Christ will make you stronger when He is in control.

Set Your Limits Ahead of Time

Use these questions to set your limits:

1. How far would I go if Jesus Christ were sitting next to me? (Hebrews 4:13)
2. What would a person I respect think of me? (1 Timothy 4:12)
3. If we break up, can I look the other person in the eye? (Acts 24:16)

4. Do I feel guilty? (Psalms 38:4)
5. Does it turn me on sexually? (1 Peter 2:11)
6. Would I want my parents to see what I am doing? (Colossians 3:20)
7. Would I want my future husband/wife doing this now? (Hebrews 13:4)

Communicate Your Limits

"I know he (or she) will want to make out, and I don't know what to do."

If you think there might be a misunderstanding between you and your date on this, *talk about it.* That relieves the tension and protects you from awkward situations. Hopefully as the relationship deepens there will be more freedom for open discussion of each partner's standards. But there definitely needs to be an understanding now. If you feel your date is more aggressive than you wish, be loving but firm. Clearly state your limits.[6] If the problem continues, break off the relationship immediately.

Avoid Tempting Situations

Note that there are times when you are more vulnerable than others. At these times you can easily ignore your limits:

- After 11 P.M.
- After an emotional event (you have a fight with your parents, your team loses a big game, you have a fight with each other, you get a bad grade).
- After special occasions (prom, birthday, homecoming).
- After spending time with friends who have lower standards.
- At certain places (alone, in the car, in the bedroom).
- While dressed sexily (tight sweaters or T-shirts, tight jeans, low-cut and loose dresses).
- After going certain places (sexy movie, wild party).

• After praying late and alone.[7]

Date Creatively

The success or failure of your relationship hinges on your ability to do things together and to communicate. When you date creatively, the options for temptation are limited. See our book *Dating: Picking (and Being) a Winner* to get good ideas on how you can date creatively.

Once you have come this far on the road to determining your sexual standards, only one thing remains to be done: Remember your destination. Your destination is tied up in two questions. Instead of asking yourself, "How far is too far?" ask

1. How far can I go to bring glory to Jesus Christ through my life? (1 Thessalonians 4:7)
2. How far can I go to help my date get closer to Jesus Christ? (1 Thessalonians 4:9)

Memorize these two questions and answer them now so that when you are tempted to go too far (and you will be tempted!), you'll know what to do and what not to do.

ACTION SECTION

1. On a scale of 1 to 10 where would you place yourself?

1	2	3	4	5	6	7	8	9	10
Holding Hands									Intercourse

On a scale of 1 to 10 where would you like to be?

1	2	3	4	5	6	7	8	9	10
Holding Hands									Intercourse

2. If you have gone further than is right, confess that to the Lord and ask forgiveness. Then ask forgiveness from the other person. (Follow the steps in chapter 11.) If you haven't ever done anything wrong sexually, thank the Lord for sparing you the pain.

3.   Using this chapter and the questions on setting limits, write down how far you will go and why.

MY SEXUAL LIMITS

Intercourse _____

_____

_____

_____

Petting _____

_____

_____

_____

Going beyond the other person's limits _____

_____

_____

Intensive kissing _____

_____

_____

_____

Kissing _____

_____

_____

_____

Holding Hands _____

_____

_____

_____

4.   Memorize these two questions.   The Lord will use these questions to remind you what to do when you get in a tight situation.

(1)   How far can I go to bring glory to Jesus Christ through my life?

(2)   How far can I go to help my date get closer to Jesus Christ?

6

What If I'm Pressured? ♥

What if your boyfriend or girlfriend pressures you to go beyond the limits you have set for yourself? What do you do when you're pressured to have sex?

Let's go back to the date at the beginning of chapter 5 — your first special date. Watch how the pressure increases. When you call to ask her out and she says yes, all kinds of exciting thoughts go through your mind — where you will go, what you will do on your date; then you jump quickly to what you want to do with her *after* your date.

The time arrives. You pick her up. You begin by *holding hands*. It's wonderful. (And it turns on the pressure valve.) But you quickly move on to *super-holding hands*. That's where you begin to rub her fingers and she rubs yours, and she runs her fingers up and down your arm. Now you're still looking cool on the outside, but on the inside you are screaming "Yeeeoooow." (The pressure is building rapidly.)

Then you carefully ease into *kissing*. That's really fun at first, but you want more! (The pressure increases.) So you go to *super-kissing* (the Roto-Rooter type). Now you are hot, so you move to *caressing*. (Almost too much pressure to handle.) Then from caressing to *super-caressing*. (You're about to bust apart.)

Then you move to *etc*. And from etc. to *super-etc*. Then one of you tries to stop. But the other one doesn't want to stop. So you go on. You get into arguments over this, then fights. You break up.

But you can't stand to be apart, so you kiss and make up. As soon as you get back together, you are in each other's arms. You grope at each other after an especially long kiss.

Sometimes you pray fervently, asking God to help you stop, but you're in each other's arms and over your heads in pressure!

What started out as fun and excitement has now become emotional torment. You can't resist the pressure! Whether your date applies the pressure to you or your emotions lay it on you — there's always pressure.

The writer of Proverbs describes this pressure:

> I was looking out the window of my house one day, and saw a simple-minded lad, a young man lacking common sense, walking at twilight down the street to the house of this wayward girl . . . She approached him . . . dressed seductively . . . She put her arms around him and kissed him . . . "I was just coming to look for you and here you are . . . Come on, let's take our fill of love until morning" . . . So she seduced him with her pretty speech, and her coaxing until he yielded to her. He couldn't resist her flattery (Proverbs 7:6-21, TLB).

SMOOTH LINES BUILD PRESSURE

That same type of pressure is either on you now or will be soon. Both guys and girls use smooth lines to pressure each other. Which of these lines have you heard?

"Everybody else is doing it." Think of it this way: If 99 percent of the people in your class were getting cancer, would you want it too? "Hey, everybody else is really getting into it. C'mon, get some cancer."

Who cares if "everybody" else is doing it?! That doesn't make it right for you!

"If you love me, you'll let me." Guys use this one a lot. If your boyfriend does this, manufacture a great big tear in the corner of your left eye and let it roll down your cheek (about two inches). Make your lip quiver. (Girls, your ability to do this is amazing.) Then say softly, "If you really love *me*, you won't ask." That puts the pressure back where it belongs.

If a girl tries this one on you, guys, tell her you like her and you like babies too, but you just don't have the money to pay for one (figure about $6,000 the first year).

Truthfully, if your boyfriend (or girlfriend) really loved you, he (or she) wouldn't ask.

"But I can't help myself." Translated that means, "Just like I need food, air and water, I need sex." You can't live without the first three, but you can live without sex. If you satisfy your sexual desires in a dating relationship, you're just using the other person — or being used.

Look at it another way. When you're furious at your kid brother and you want to toss him from a third-story window, you resist for many reasons — like not wanting to spend the rest of your life in jail! Your date can resist the impulse to make love, too.

If you are dating a person who has so little self-control, all you need to say is, "If you're so weak, I don't need to date you, because I want to have my life under control."

"But it feels so good." Yes, but for how long? What feels good for a few minutes may cause you to feel miserable for years. Are you prepared to live with the guilt and the flashbacks? And a child? If you have the Spirit of God in you, you'll feel rotten even before you finish.

"Practice makes perfect." The argument goes like this: "We need experience so when we get married we'll know what we're doing." But you can count on this: Your system

will always work! God made your body to respond physically.   A study of approximatcly 2000 women concluded,
"Neither delayed marriage nor lack of previous sexual experience is a hindrance to a woman's good sexual adjustment in
marriage."[1]

If you choose to do it God's way — in marriage —
then your undamaged emotions, your guilt-free mind and your
pure heart can be brought into the marriage relationship along
with sex.   You'll have years of practice to make it perfect,
too!

You've probably heard all of these lines and many
more, like . . .

"It's good exercise." Ride a bike.

"Oh, please just this once." How many times does it
take to lose your virginity?

"You owe it to me." Really?   Who pays the bills
when you get sick?   Or who is going to marry you if you get
pregnant?

"If you don't, somebody else will." That's a threat!
There's not much love and romance in a threat.   That person
is only going to hurt someone.   Make sure it's not you.

"It will make us close." Remember sex outside of
marriage is a wedge that drives you apart.   But sex in marriage is a rope that binds you together.

"We can use contraceptives and not get pregnant."
With over 1 million teenage pregnancies each year, somebody
isn't getting the message.   No contraceptive is 100 percent
effective.

"It's OK as long as we don't go all the way." Going
all the way isn't the only way to disobey God! And real soon
things will get so hot that you'll lose control . . . and your
virginity.

"I won't get you pregnant"/"I'm not going to get
pregnant." No one can make that guarantee.   Even if the
other person won't hold you liable, you're responsible for the
child. Both of you are.

"If it happens, it happens." With that approach, it *will*
happen!   The person who wants it to happen will wear you

down, and eventually you will give in.

"But we're so much in love." This is the one that wipes out the most people. In the heat of passion, it sounds so right, so romantic. But when you give in to that pressure and have sex together, what happens after that?

- You lose *restraint.* So you do it over and over. You can't seem to go back to where you were before.
- You lose *respect.* Instead of holding that person in high esteem, now you see all of that person's flaws and weaknesses. You get irritated with each other a lot.
- You live with *guilt.* You know that no matter how much you try to justify it, your conscience bothers you.
- You are *suspicious.* "Am I the only one?"
- You are *afraid.* "What if he/she breaks up with me?"
- You are *anxious.* "What if I/she get(s) pregnant?"
- You get *depressed.* When it doesn't work out (and it rarely ever does), you plunge into depression.
- You get pregnant.

All of the pressure lines are lies! They promise satisfaction. They deliver guilt, confusion, bitter relationships and unwanted babies. These lines apply pressure that you don't need.

LIFE PROBLEMS THAT BUILD PRESSURE

The pressure is *tremendous.* And that's just the pressure from your date. What about the pressure you feel on the inside that causes you to "cave in" to sexual advances?

Revenge

"I hate my parents. I'm hurt and I'm mad. What will hurt them the most is for me to lose my virginity. That's what I'll do."

Let's say your parents are 100 percent wrong and you are 100 percent right (which is rarely the case). Who are you hurting? Your parents, for sure. But, even worse, you're hurting yourself.

- You wipe out your dating relationship with "angry sex." Now you have *two* bad relationships.
- Your anger leads to bad decisions that lead to more and more problems. For example, sex leads to pregnancy which, for many people, leads to the tragedy of abortion.
- You hate yourself and feel rejected.

A suggestion: Tell God how angry you are with your parents, but that you will obey Him and them. Then follow the directions of Ephesians 6:1-3: "Children, obey your parents in the Lord, for this is right. 'Honor your father and mother' — which is the first commandment with a promise — 'that it may go well with you and that you may enjoy long life on the earth.'"

Popularity

"I want to date, and the only way to get and keep a guy (girl) is to put out on a date. I'll do that if it means I can go out."

This shows that you have a crippling need to be popular. There is nothing wrong with wanting to go out, but to use the precious gift of your sexuality to do that poses serious problems. Why?

- If you get a guy (girl) by putting out, you keep the relationship going by putting out. Your date is going out with you only for what he (or she) can get out of you, not because he even likes you or cares to build a relationship.
- You have to be "sexually ready" every time. In a survey of students, the question was asked, "Have there been times when you've been on a date and had sexual contact even though you really did not

feel like it?" Forty-three percent of the guys and 65 percent of the girls answered yes. That's no way to date.[2]

- You make popularity your god. Anything (or anyone) more important to you than the true and living God is your real god. If you're willing to disobey God in order to be popular, then popularity is your god.

A suggestion: Decide to make Jesus first in your life. Follow the advice of Jesus: "Seek first His kingdom" knowing that "all of these [other] things [including dates] will be added to you" (Matthew 6:33, NASB).

Acceptance

"All of my friends are having sex, and I really feel out of it because I'm still a virgin."

To take the pressure off, realize that everybody else is *not* doing it! Thousands of students are choosing not to have sex before marriage. You are not strange if you choose not to have sex.

A suggestion: See yourself the way God sees you . . .

- Unique — God hasn't made you to be like every one else or to do what everyone else does (see Psalm 139:13-16).
- Loved — God loves you deeply (see Romans 5:8; 8:38,39).
- Accepted — God, not the opposite sex, gives you the acceptance you need. Others may reject you, and you may even reject yourself, but God accepts you like you are (see Ephesians 1:5).

Receive the uniqueness, love and acceptance He offers to you right now.

Security

"I'm afraid that if I don't have sex he (or she) will leave me."

Have you ever watched a couple walk down the hall at school, clinging to each other so tight that it looks like they have each other in a vice grip? The only reason she'll let loose is if she sees another girl look at her man. She'll go over and claw that girl's eyes out, then get set to regrip. That's insecurity.

If this is your response, then you are motivated by a paralyzing fear that leads to deeper and deeper insecurity.

A suggestion: The Bible says 365 times to "Fear not" (one for each day of the year). Love replaces fear. The apostle John expressed it this way: "There is no fear in love; but perfect love casts out fear, because fear involves punishment, and the one who fears is not perfected in love [is insecure]" (1 John 4:18,19, NASB). Ask God to take away your fear and replace it with the security of His love.

The areas of love, acceptance and security are dealt with extensively by Josh McDowell in *His Image . . . My Image* (Here's Life Publishers).

So how do you handle the pressure? We have given some suggestions along the way, but now look at one suggestion that, when understood and followed, will cause you to beat the pressure.

RESIST TEMPTATION

The sexual pressure you feel is a temptation. James 1:13-15 explains temptation:

> When tempted, no one should say, "God is tempting me." For God cannot be tempted by evil, nor does he tempt anyone; but each one is tempted when, by his own evil desire, he is dragged away and enticed. Then, after desire has conceived, it gives birth to sin; and sin, when it is full-grown, gives birth to death.

The dictionary defines temptation as "the act of enticement to do wrong, by the promise of pleasure or gain."[3] Amazing! Temptation pressures you to be bad by promising you something good. That's what every one of those pressure lines does to you.

In order to resist sexual temptation, you need to know some things about it.

Temptation will pressure you. James doesn't say, "When tempted you will not be pressured." You will always be pressured. The question is, are you going to give in to the pressure?

Temptation doesn't come from God. James does tell us, "nor does he [God] tempt anyone" (verse 13). God never puts pressure on you to sin. Satan does that. He is a "roaring lion" trying to eat you alive with temptation (1 Peter 5:8). In fact, God is the one who causes you to overcome temptation.

Giving in to temptation is your choice. James states clearly, "But each one is tempted when, by his own evil desire . . ." (verse 14). No pressure outside of you is powerful enough to force you to sin. You give in to it when *you* decide to. Giving in to temptation can't be blamed on someone else. You are responsible.

Temptation always follows the same cycle. Let's say you are a fish. While swimming one day you see this absolutely gorgeous worm dangling down in the water. You swim up and look at the worm. "Hmmm, looks pretty good, but I'd better not. I remember my dad told me once not to eat strange worms. Sometimes they have a hook in them, tied to a string which is tied to a pole." So you swim away. But now you have that big, fat, juicy worm on your mind. You start thinking about how good it might taste, so you swim back and look at it again. "Well, it looks delicious, but . . . better not." Then you swim around it a few times. The more you swim the better it looks. "Gee, I'm hungry." Now you can see yourself eating it and how good it will taste. You can't stand it anymore — chomp — you bite it. And you are hooked!

What a graphic picture of how you can get sucked into temptation. The word *entice* (verse 14) is a fishing word. A fisherman baits his line to attract the fish — he's made his line enticing.

The Cycle of Temptation follows this pattern:

The Lure ——————————

The Bait ——————————

The Bite ——————————

The Bloat——————

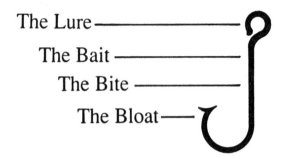

• *The lure.* The worm is dropped in the water. You become curious. You let your thoughts go. Those thoughts make you feel good. You enjoy the lines, the teasing, the looks at each other. You decide you will park. You're not going to make out — just enjoy the radio, the city lights, and being together. You have just been "tempted . . . by [your] evil desire" (verse 14).

• *The bait.* Now you are not just thinking about the bait, but *actively pursuing* it with all of your might. Everything inside of you is attracted to that bait. You want it — bad! And you are determined to get it. Why? Because you know that if you get it you will be satisfied — "Satisfaction guaranteed." This will give you everything you've always wanted in life. If you have this guy or girl, your whole life will be complete. So you say yes to the smooth lines. You give in to the pressure. You have just been "dragged away and enticed" (verse 14).

• *The bite.* When you can stand it no longer, you bite the bait. You swallow the worm. At this point you have moved from temptation to sin. You give in to the pressure. You lower your standards or you go all the way. You get what you want. James puts it this way: "Then after desire has conceived, it gives birth to sin" (verse 15). The desire to have what you want grows inside of you until it comes out in your life as sin.

• *The bloat.* Now that you are hooked, that worm

grows inside of you. You want to get free, because you know you are hooked, but you can't get satisfied either. Once you lower your standards, once you go all the way, it's as if you can't help yourself. Sin grows. That's what James means when he says, "Sin, when it is full grown . . ." (verse 15). Now giving in to temptation becomes a habit. And you are under the control of sex.

• *The bitter end.* You are hooked. You can wiggle and squirm, but it's only a matter of time. You're as good as dead. Giving in to your sexual desires to satisfy yourself, rather than waiting to satisfy God, leads to spiritual death. James says that you have reached the point where "sin . . . gives birth to death" (verse 15). You've been had!

When you decide to give in to the pressure and go out after the bait of satisfying your sexual desire, then you're as good as gone. The solution, then, is to resist the temptation to bite the bait no matter how juicy it looks. How do you do that? Follow "The Fish's Handbook of Bait Resistance" to get unhooked and stay unhooked.

Rejoice. Now that's a strange solution. But it shows how creative God is. When Satan tempts you with lust, God tells you to rejoice in that. James 1:2 says, "Consider it pure joy, my brothers, whenever you face trials of many kinds." Sexual pressure is a trial that God will use in your life to build your character. So when you are experiencing sexual pressure say, "I'm glad, Lord, for this opportunity to trust You."

Resist with endurance. When you are out of shape and then work out, you get sore muscles. Doctors say that when you work out, a whole new network of blood vessels develops to feed the muscles and take care of the extra demand. This network doesn't open one vessel at a time, but all at once. While you have been enduring the sore muscles, this network that has been developing like mad to meet the need suddenly opens up.

James suggests the same idea when facing trials and temptations: "For when the way is rough, your patience has a chance to grow. So let it grow, and don't try to squirm out

of your problems" (James 1:3,4, TLB).   Sexually, resist the
smooth lines. It may be hard. You may feel like you can't
hold out, but you will reach a point where you have resisted
enough that you will have a whole network of spiritual blood
vessels to give you new strength.   When you do, you build
endurance that makes you stronger — "mature and complete."

Recognize the lie. When these pressure lines are used
on you, and you know that they are not from God, don't go
near the bait. When James says, "Do not be deceived," what
he means is *don't lie to yourself!* Be honest — with your
thoughts, with your emotions, with your decisions and with
your body.

Rely on Jesus. You have probably given in to temptation so many times that you certainly know by now that
you are not the solution. Jesus is. That's what James means
when he says, "Every good and perfect gift is from above"
(James 1:17).   You need to be like a mouse when he's
chased by a woman with a broom — he doesn't have his eye
on the broom; he's looking for his hole. Keep *your* eyes on
Jesus.   James 1:5 tells you how: "If any of you lacks wisdom, he should ask God, who gives generously to all without
finding fault, and it will be given to him." Wisdom is seeing
the sexual pressure from God's perspective, having His insight into it. To get God's insight, read Proverbs 5, 6 and 7.

Redirect your actions. When someone puts the pressure on you, take action. First, get rid of the temptation.
James says, "Get rid of all moral filth" (James 1:21). What
is tempting you? Whatever it is — a magazine, a person, a
movie, a video, a thought — get it away from you.   Then,
replace it with a new set of desires — God's desires.

The book of James challenges you to "humbly accept
the word of God planted in you" (James 1:21). You have
Jesus in you and His Word will give you strength. When the
Word of God is in your heart — read, memorized and stud-
ied — it comes on like gang-busters, fighting against temptation and fighting for the truth. No temptation can stand
against the truth. So memorize Scripture. (Start with 1
Corinthians 10:13.)   Then obey it. James says, "Do not

merely listen to the word, but do what it says" (James 1:22).

As you follow these directions, you will get free from the hook of sexual pressure. That's what James promises "the man who looks into the perfect law that gives freedom" (James 1:25). Jesus is the "perfect law." He sets you free from sexual pressure!

ACTION SECTION

1. Write down the lines used on you. How can you respond to them?

LINES   HOW I CAN RESPOND

(1) _____   _____

_____   _____

(2) _____   _____

_____   _____

(3) _____   _____

_____   _____

2. What lines have you used? What was your motive?

LINES   MOTIVE

(1) _____   _____

_____   _____

(2) _____   _____

_____   _____

(3) _____   _____

_____   _____

3. What is one "life problem" that puts pressure on you? (See page 89.)

_____

What practical steps can you take to overcome it?

_____

_____

_____

    4. Think of the most recent tempting situation you've been in. How did you get hooked?

_____

_____

_____

    5. Using the solution steps given to resist temptation, how can you overcome the pressure in the future?

Rejoice. _____

_____

Resist with endurance. _____

_____

Recognize the lie. _____

_____

Rely on Jesus. _____

_____

Redirect your actions. _____

_____

7

Is Lust Abnormal? ♥

I see a lot of beautiful, sexy women. Is looking at them lust?"

"I fantasize about my sexual involvement with him. I enjoy it and feel bad at the same time. Why?"

"Can't a guy admire a girl's looks without committing a terrible sin?"

"Can't a girl daydream about a special guy?"

"What's the problem with looking at porn magazines?"

When you think about the opposite sex — is it love or is it lust?

"I love oranges!" Barry exclaims. "In the winter, when they are in season, there is nothing better than eating a good orange. When they're not in season, I think about them until they are. I like fresh-squeezed orange juice; I like oranges in sections; I like peeling them and eating them whole. I love oranges!

"Or do I lust after oranges? Am I really concerned about that orange, or am I using that orange to satisfy my physical appetite?"

When you think about the opposite sex, you can tell whether it is love or lust. Do you really care for the other person, or do you use that person to satisfy your sexual desires?

— Love always waits to give.

— Lust never waits to get.

Jesus explained lust clearly in Matthew 5:27,28: "You have heard that it was said, 'Do not commit adultery.' But I tell you that anyone who looks at a woman lustfully has already committed adultery with her in his heart."

That is a strong statement. Obviously Jesus didn't take lust lightly. The word He uses in Greek is *epithumia*. *Epi* means "over" and *thumos* means "passion." Lust means "overpassion." (Now you can say you know a foreign language.) Lust is a burning desire for the opposite sex.

God has blessed you with your sexual desires. He has special plans for you to use those desires within marriage. That is normal. So when you look at a person and say, "Now there's an attractive person," that's cool.

But sexual desires that come from *lust* are not from God. If you think, *I wonder what he (or she) looks like undressed*, you're into lust. From there your thoughts run out of control until you imagine anything from messing around to having sexual intercourse with a person, and those thoughts are wrong.

HOT TO TROT

Let's see how guys get lured into lust.

You walk into one of those "quick stop" stores. Dozens of magazines of naked women are behind the counter, and it's definitely not because of their literary value.

Jesus said that a man doesn't have to have intercourse with a woman outside of marriage to commit adultery — he only has to *look* at a woman (Matthew 5:27,28). Lust begins

with your eyes. Those pictures go from

YOUR EYES

TO YOUR BRAIN

TO YOUR BODY

Guys, if you see a girl with her blouse gaping open in class, what do you do? Look, swallow hard, take another look, get a tingling sensation, stare. Later that night all you can think of is her. Your imagination runs wild. You don't have to touch her to get stimulated. A couple of good looks and your mind can think of nothing else.

One of the biggest areas where guys get their eyes full is pornography. In a survey of high school guys, 99 percent of them answered yes to the question "Have you ever read or looked at sexy books or magazines?"[1] That doesn't make you a pervert; we're all curious creatures. But it does fill your eyes and mind with the wrong images. That's dangerous. One friend of ours has had tremendous struggles with sexual impurity after getting married. He loves his wife, but lusts after other women. It happens, he says, because he filled his mind with pornography in high school. Pornography captured his mind.

And the same thing has happened to some women as well. Pornography for women has become very prevalent over the past few years.

Carried to the extreme, continual exposure to pornography can lead to rape, child abuse, torture, perversion, even murder. It's a wrong turn onto a dead-end street.

FANTASY LAND

Girls, maybe you have had some thoughts like this:

- "He's a hunk. I sure would like to snuggle up to him."
- "I dreamed about him holding me in his arms and kissing me. I woke up before we went all the way."
- "Oh, wow, would I like to get him to lust after me."

No you wouldn't, because those are fantasies in your mind, and it's not that way in reality. If you live in a fantasy world and move into the reality of a relationship, you get disappointed.

Here's how most girls operate — it's all in your mind.

ROMANTIC EYES

➔ FANTASY MIND

➔ SEXY BODY

When you give expression to those sexual feelings and get a guy to lust after you, here's how that lustful guy thinks of you: "She's easy. I can go to bed with her without much work and leave her when I'm done." Yet if you ask that same guy what kind of girl he wants to marry, he will tell you that he wants to marry a virgin. Talk about a double standard!

When you encourage a guy to lust after you, then all he cares about is your body. He doesn't care about you, your feelings or your needs.

When your sensual imagination expresses itself through your body, it usually begins with the way you dress. Picture yourself in last summer's bathing suit. Remember the colors, the cost and the cut of it? Now picture yourself walking around at the pool. What do you think guys were looking at when they looked at you? Your brown eyes? Sure!

You stand in front of the mirror dressing for school and you decide to unbutton one more button. You tell yourself, "Nobody can see." Then in the hall between first and second periods you drop your English book, so you bend over to pick it up. What happens to your blouse? Well, you might as well have the school marching band come by and blast out "Da, da, da, da — Presenting . . . !"

Some girls don't even realize what this kind of action does to guys. But girls, you need to know — it drives them crazy. If that's what you want to do, you will be successful. But very quickly he'll drop you for someone new. You are much too wonderful for that! God has a better plan for you.

LUST TEST

Whether you're a guy or a girl, take this test to determine how serious your lusting problem is.

On a scale of 1 to 10:

1. How often do you stare a girl or guy down, then let your imagination run?

1	2	3	4	5	6	7	8	9	10
Never									Constantly

2. How often is your mind overwhelmed by your impure thoughts?

1	2	3	4	5	6	7	8	9	10
Never									Constantly

3. Are these experiences happening more and more

frequently?

1	2	3	4	5	6	7	8	9	10
No									Yes

4. If you knew you would not get caught, would you fulfill your lustful desires?

1	2	3	4	5	6	7	8	9	10
No									Yes

A BIG FIRE

How does lust — that burning desire for the opposite sex — affect you?

Let's say that instead of "Fire Prevention Week" at your school, you have "Fire Education Week." They teach you how to build a fire in your bedroom wastebasket. Every time you turn on the TV someone is enjoying a bedroom fire in their bedroom wastebasket. All of the billboards have happy, sharp people sitting around the wastebasket fire. Soon even the younger kids are building those fires in their bedrooms. What effect do you think this would have on house fires?[2] Your whole city would soon be up in flames.

Proverbs 6:25,27 explains how lust is like a fire: "Do not lust in your heart after her beauty or let her captivate you with her eyes. Can a man scoop fire into his lap without his clothes being burned?" Picture your eyes catching on fire, then spreading to your mind, then consuming your body. Fire begins with your eyes. That is why Jesus said that all a person has to do is "look . . . lustfully and he has already committed adultery with her in his heart." Jesus also said, "The eye is the lamp of the body. If your eyes are good, your whole body will be full of light" (Matthew 6:22).

Your eyes are bombarded with lust material all of the time. One youth leader expressed it this way (see if what he says isn't what you experience): "We live in a sex-saturated society that constantly bombards all of us with erotic stimuli. Suggestive poses and near-nude bodies are just a glance away. 'Come-on' eyes peer at us from colorful, provocative ads on television, in magazines, and on billboards."[3]

If lust catches fire in your eyes, then it spreads to your mind, and your mind is your most important sex organ. If the fire of lust smolders there, you are in trouble. The apostle Paul expressed it this way: "But I am afraid that as the serpent deceived Eve by his cunning, your thoughts will be led astray from a sincere and pure devotion to Christ" (2 Corinthians 11:3). How did the serpent deceive Eve? He got her to lust after the forbidden fruit. The lustful thought smoldered in her mind until she gave in to it. Is your mind consumed with sexual thoughts, desires and dreams?

When lust smolders in your mind, it's only a matter of time until it explodes into your body. Your body is blazing with lust, not because of what you have done, necessarily, but because of what you have seen and what you have thought about what you have seen.

So now you want to put the fire out. How do you do it?

EXTINGUISHING THE FIRE

You are messing around with some matches and that starts a fire in your room. You don't realize it at first, but then you smell smoke. PANIC! Now what do you do?

The steps for putting out a fire in your room are the same ones you use to extinguish lust.

Find Out Where the Fire Is

You follow the smoke until you find that the fire is in your wastebasket. Now follow the smoke of your lust to see where the burning desires are. Use this "Lust Meter" to help you.[4]

When thinking about the opposite sex, at what point will thoughts of sexual intercourse race across your imagination? At what point do you look at the opposite sex lustfully? It's at that point that you need to douse the fire. Put a circle around the number that describes where you are.

LUST METER

10   Sexual intercourse
9   Oral Sex
8   Heavy Petting
7   Petting
6   Necking
5   Long Kiss
4   Goodnight kiss
3   Holding hands
2   Being together
1   Looking at a person

Discover How Bad the Fire Is[5]

Now that you know the fire is in your wastebasket, how bad is it? Is it just this week's school paper? No big deal. Or is your whole room going up in flames (your stereo is melting, your newest clothes are engulfed in flames and your yearbook is on fire)? Real big deal!

How bad is the burning desire of lust in your life?

Lustful thoughts. If lust has gotten past your eyes and into your mind, that's where you determine how bad it is. Your mind is like a computer. The problem is input. The old saying goes, "garbage in — garbage out." If you put garbage into your mind, eventually garbage comes out. And the more garbage you put into your mind, the more garbage comes out. As we mentioned before, Jesus pointed this out: "The good man brings good things out of the good stored up in his heart, and the evil man brings evil things out of the evil stored up in his heart. For out of the overflow of his heart his mouth speaks" (Luke 6:45).

This "garbage-in" stuff fuels your fire:

- television
- books
- magazines
- posters
- movies
- music videos
- conversations
- music

Although nothing is wrong with any of these means of communication, they are often used to influence your mind negatively toward lust. If you feed your mind trash, then trash will come out.

Like the trash that catches fire, lust gets progressively hotter and hotter.

Excuses. Have you heard about the frog who was put in a pot of water on a stove, and the heat was turned up? If the heat had been turned up quickly, instinctively he would have leaped out to safety. But the heat was turned up slowly; the frog was boiled to death. He didn't even know what happened to him.

You do the same thing to yourself when you rationalize your impure, lustful thoughts. Do you ever find yourself using these excuses?

- "I'm only human."
- "No one is perfect."
- "I've tried and tried and tried but I can't win."
- "After all, God created me with these desires."
- "When I get married it will be all right."
- "This is just what I want to do right now."
- "I don't feel guilty."
- "A few mistakes now won't hurt that much."
- "Most of my friends are worse off than me."
- "One of my leaders said it was OK."[6]

Compromise. It's not one big forest fire of passion that gets you, but it's the little brush fires. The little compromises get the fire hotter and hotter.

To illustrate this to his son, one student's dad had him drive a nail in a tree every time his son had a lustful thought. After a month they went out and looked at the tree. It was full of nails and dying.

Loss of control. Now, instead of you controlling lust, lust controls you. You want to stop, but you can't. You want to change, but you don't. And now lust is burning you up.

Downfall. When this goes on long enough, a pattern

develops in your life:

> Sow a thought → Reap an action.
>   Sow an action → Reap a habit.
>   Sow a habit → Reap a lifestyle.
>   Sow a lifestyle → Reap a destiny.

How bad is the fire of lust inside of you?

Put the Fire Out

When the fire is burning out of control in your room, you need to grab the fire extinguisher and *blast!* And keep on blasting until it's out. That's what you do to burning lust as well.

But *you* can't do that. Only Jesus can! You've tried again and again, and you've failed again and again. Your efforts are no match for the power of sin. That's like attacking a forest fire with a squirt gun. Recognize that Jesus is *"The Extinguisher."* He said, "Apart from me you can do nothing" (John 15:15). Ask the Lord to put out the fire. Then follow what He tells you to do.

He will be "The Extinguisher" in the three places the fire of your lust is burning — your eyes, your brain and your body. To cooperate with Him in putting the fire out, you need to follow the steps below.

Your eyes. Job 31:1 says, "I made a covenant with my eyes not to look lustfully at a girl."

Do like Job and make a commitment with your eyes.

1. *Avoid the second look.* The first look is natural. With the second look you fuel the fire. Focus on the color of the person's eyes, not on the shape of the body.

2. *Dress properly.* This keeps you and others from lust. Dress realizing that Jesus is going with you on your date.

3. *Choose carefully what you see.* TV, movies, music videos, books, magazines and posters can all fuel the fire of lust. Discipline yourself to watch and read only what will strengthen you.

4. *Plan your leisure time.* When you have nothing to do, you can get into trouble. Decide beforehand how you will spend a free evening.

Your brain. Ephesians 4:22,23 tells us, "You were taught, with regard to your former way of life, to put off your old self, which is being corrupted by its deceitful desires; to be made new in the attitude of your minds."

You can renew your mind by replacing the lustful thoughts in there now with the thoughts of God. From your chemistry class you know that liquid forces gas out of a test tube. In the same way, God's more powerful thoughts from Scripture can force the lustful thoughts out of your mind. When your mind begins to wander, immediately replace your lustful thoughts with God's pure thoughts.

You can do that in many ways — Christian music, magazines, books, good movies and TV, and positive conversations. The most significant way is through *Scripture memory.* To memorize Scripture:

1. *Decide to memorize at least one verse per week.* That's fifty-two a year. Start with these: Romans 12:1,2; Psalm 51:10; Colossians 3:1-3; Psalm 119:9,11; 1 Corinthians 10:13; Philippians 4:8.

2. *Memorize word perfect.* Don't make up your own translation.

3. *Think about the verse.* This is called meditation. What does the verse mean to you? What is God saying to you?

4. *Apply the verse to your life.* "As a result of this verse, I will . . ."

5. *Review.* Go over the new verse every day for two months. Then once a week after that.

Your body. The Bible challenges you: "Beloved, I beseech you as aliens and exiles to abstain from the passions of the flesh that wage war against your soul" (1 Peter 2:11, RSV). That verse says to *control your body.*

If you follow the steps on how to control your eyes and your mind, then your body will come under control. You will begin to experience victory.

Realize that your sexual desires are strong, and that you will fail occasionally. You're normal. When you do mess up, simply pick up your fire extinguisher and start blasting.

If, for some reason, your body continues to be out of control, then talk to an older person whom you trust. Remember, God is committed to bringing the fire of lust in your life under His control. Only Jesus can extinguish your burning "overpassion." Keep turning it over to Him.

ACTION SECTION

1.   Define lust. _____

_____

2.   Describe how lust affects you. _____

_____

3.   Take the "Lust Test" on page 103.
4.   Where are you on the "Lust Meter" on page 106?_____

5.   What do you do to fuel the fire of your lust? (See page 106.)

_____

_____

6.   What specific steps are you going to take to put the fire out? (Be very prayerful, honest and specific.)
In your eyes
(1)_____
(2)_____
In your mind
(1)_____
(2)_____
In your body
(1)_____
(2)_____

8

What About Masturbation? ♥

*F*or years masturbation has controlled him. He discovered it by accident when he was twelve. Soon
it became a habit. He enjoys it, telling himself that it's
healthy to release his sexual desires. Yet he hates it, feeling
guilty about what he's doing. He knows deep down that it's
wrong, but he doesn't know how to stop. It's a constant
battle. Sometimes he feels like he is going to explode.

This is a struggle that haunts many young people,
guys and girls. Statistics vary, but all agree that more than
60 percent of the females and more than 90 percent of the
males have been involved in masturbation — stimulating
one's own sexual organs to achieve an orgasm — at some
time in their lives.

Little wonder! Your insides feel like the radiator of
a car. The more the heat rises in the motor, the more the
pressure builds in the radiator, until it finally explodes.

Does this describe you? If it does, you probably don't understand what's going on inside of you — much less how to handle it. The purpose of this chapter is to help you with that.

THE MASTURBATION MYTHS

All kinds of jokes and stories are told about masturbation. They only confuse the facts. As a result of these myths you probably have some wrong ideas about masturbation.

"I'm weird." As we mentioned above, a majority of people have been involved in masturbation at some time in their lives. A person is not weird if he or she has had this experience — or if he or she hasn't. Far too many young people believe they are the only ones who have done this. If you have, you're not alone.

"I'll be permanently damaged." No evidence supports the old wives' tales that masturbation injures your health or mental abilities. In fact, there are no known physically or mentally damaging effects of masturbation.

"I'm dirty." Some parents communicate that sex is "The Big No-No." Children learn that it is not to be talked about.

"Shame on you."

"Nice girls don't do that."

"We don't talk about that."

So instead of growing up feeling that their sexuality is healthy, those children get the message that sex is dirty. This unhealthy view of sex tells them that they are dirty when they masturbate. They, personally, are condemned, rather than dealing with the guilt of the act itself.

"This is my biggest problem." Many young people allow masturbation to become the central focus of their lives. Because of their fear or guilt, the problem is reinforced and more pressure is added. Because they have not conquered masturbation, many carry a nagging guilt and a constant attitude of defeat.

Masturbation is not *"The Big Problem."* Thinking

that way puts the focus on the negative and on continuous failure, leading to giving in and giving up. How much better to take the positive approach (which is the ultimate solution to this issue anyway) and channel that same energy into developing a dynamic relationship with Jesus Christ.

Have you been trapped in one of these myths? If you have, you can breathe a sigh of relief, because you are not weird, damaged, dirty or a failure. Whew! That takes some of the pressure off your radiator.

IS MASTURBATION A SIN?

People have different views about this question. Some say:

- Masturbation is obviously a sin, because it is a form of sex outside of marriage.
- It is not a sin, but it is not ideal either.
- It is good, because it relieves sexual tension.

We believe that the Bible teaches a different approach from any of these.

Nowhere in the Scripture is masturbation mentioned. Some people have condemned masturbation as "Onanism" after Onan who "spilled [his] semen on the ground" (see Genesis 38:4-10). God struck Onan dead for what he did, but that passage has nothing to do with masturbation. The real issue was Onan's disobedience in refusing to bear children for his deceased brother, which he was bound by law to do. Nowhere does the Bible directly condemn masturbation.

On the other hand, the Bible does not say that masturbation is right. So how do you know whether it is right or wrong? By the definition of two terms: *natural release* and *masturbation*.

Natural Release

When a person goes through puberty, he or she matures sexually. The sex organs become more developed. Strong sexual feelings and tensions result.

Many guys experience *nocturnal emissions*, often called "wet dreams." A man's scxual dcsires develop strongly in adolescence. His body produces sperm and stores them in the seminal vesicles (see page 35). When they are filled, the sexual desires increase.

God designed the male's body to handle the release of sexual tension in a natural way. The seminal fluid can be released through the penis while a guy is sleeping. If this happens, it can be embarrassing, almost like he's regressed to bed wetting. If this happens to you, you don't need to be ashamed of it.[1]

If the semen is not released through masturbation or intercourse, then nocturnal emissions are inevitable. One pediatrician illustrates it vividly: "It is like a water bucket left out in the rain. After the rain has reached the top, any more water added will make it overflow. It simply cannot hold any more."[2]

Realize, though, that nocturnal emissions are regulated to some degree by your thoughts. What you think about while you're awake can affect your dreams. So follow the steps later in this chapter to keep your thoughts pure.

A girl's sexual desires differ significantly from a guy's. A woman's body doesn't build up sexual tension in the same way a guy's does, so she won't experience "wet dreams." Rather, her sex drive is more dormant. Her needs are more emotional, centering on the need to be loved. When that need is not met through strong family relationships and friendships (God's natural way of dealing with her sex drive), it can surface to the physical.

Masturbation

The only other way to experience release is through masturbation. When the sex organs develop and sexual feelings become intense, these feelings are often released by masturbation. Masturbation is called *autoeroticism*. *Auto* means "self" and *eroticism* means "sexual stimulation." Put the words together and you have "self sexual stimulation."[3]

For a man, this occurs when he is aroused by sight or

thoughts. When orgasm takes place along with mental images of nakedness or going to bed with a woman, then that's lust. And Jesus says, "You have heard that it was said, 'Do not commit adultery.' But I tell you that anyone who looks at a woman lustfully has already committed adultery with her in his heart" (Matthew 5:27,28). Masturbation is lust, and, according to Jesus, lust is wrong.

For a girl, those desires must be awakened. Because a woman's sexual desires are tied more to her emotions, she must *learn* masturbation. Rather than sights or thoughts of nakedness, it's thoughts of romance that stimulate her. Usually daydreaming about guys and imagining that they are paying attention to her draw her into sexual stimulation. Those thoughts not only make her feel good physically, but they also make her feel good emotionally. The problem is that she is trying to get her emotional needs met through lust (pleasurable fantasies) rather than through real love relationships. And lust is wrong.

Once awakened, masturbation may be even more controlling for a woman than for a man. It is more difficult for a woman to develop a strong habit of masturbation and also more difficult for her to break it.[4]

Masturbation is man's unnatural way of dealing with the sex drive.

Are you taking the pressure off God's way or man's way? Your sex drive is the normal, God-given design of any healthy man or woman. To use it God's way is great. To misuse it man's way is to miss out on God's best for you.

What's Wrong With Masturbation?

Using the definitions discussed above, then, nocturnal emission for guys and strong family relationships and friendships for girls are God's natural ways of releasing and controlling sexual tension. Masturbation is the selfish and unnatural way of sexual release. Therefore, *masturbation has no place in the life of a follower of Jesus Christ.*

It comes from lust. Masturbation takes place when you allow pictures in your mind of the opposite sex. These pictures lure you into gratifying your senses and satisfying your sexual appetite. First Peter 2:11 says, "Beloved, I beseech you as aliens and exiles to abstain from the passions of the flesh that wage war against your souls." Masturbation is a "passion of the flesh." That is wrong.

It builds on fantasy. Almost everyone indulges in sexual fantasies. One study found that people of both sexes spent up to one quarter of their time sexually fantasizing. Another study indicated that men have thoughts about sex every twenty-nine seconds. And girls read enough romantic stories in magazines and romantic novels to stimulate constant daydreams and fantasies.

The more you fantasize, the more you masturbate. The more you masturbate, the more you fantasize. But for the Christian it's not only wrong, it's not necessary. Paul writes in 2 Corinthians 10:4,5: "The weapons we fight with are not the weapons of the world. On the contrary, they have divine power to demolish strongholds . . . and we take captive every thought to make it obedient to Christ." You have the power to capture your fantasies.

It intensifies sensuality. Sensuality is an absence of restraint, like a car that barrels ahead with the accelerator pushed to the floor. Sensuality does whatever feels good, like masturbation. The apostle Paul shows where this leads: "Having lost all sensitivity, they had given themselves over to sensuality so as to indulge in every kind of impurity, with a continual lust for more" (Ephesians 4:19).

It focuses on pleasing self. Control is the ability to say no to pleasing yourself in order to please another. Masturbation pleases only one person — you. Paul tells Timothy that great stress is caused when people are "lovers of self . . . [and] lovers of pleasure rather than lovers of God" (2 Timothy 3:2,4). Masturbation is a totally self-centered act and creates more self-centeredness.

It gets you into a sexual rut. Masturbation conditions your future sexual response. When you are aroused sexually, you have mental images that stimulate you. For example, a guy has a mental image of one particularly sexy girl. So he brings up that mental image any time he wants that original turn-on as an aid in masturbation. Eventually, he finds that he cannot get turned on *unless* he has that girl in mind. That puts him in a sexual rut. Girls can get in the same rut.

This rut can be detrimental to your future sexual relationship in marriage because you have conditioned yourself for response. It will take God's power and work on your part to reprogram yourself to respond to your mate. Paul says in Romans 6:12: "Therefore do not let sin reign in your mortal body so that you obey its evil desires." God's design is for freedom, not a sexual rut.

It causes you to avoid reality. When masturbation becomes frequent, it poses many problems. One problem is that this preoccupation with satisfying yourself is an escape to cover failure at school, anxiety over problems, inadequacy around your peers, lack of friends and social life, or lack of love from your parents. You escape into your shell and masturbate frequently. But that is not God's way. Paul says that the Lord "will bring to light the things hidden in the darkness and disclose the motives of men's hearts" (1 Corinthians 4:5, NASB). To escape from reality through masturbation is not God's way.

It creates a fear of homosexual tendencies. In some people, masturbating in the presence of another person or with a group can cause a deep and irrational fear of becoming a homosexual or even add to homosexual tendencies and practices.

It puts you in bondage. When masturbation becomes a habit, it controls you. Then you are a slave to it. Randy Alcorn, author of *Christians in the Wake of the Sexual Revolution*, says:

> Masturbation can become an obsessive and enslaving habit fueling and refueling the fire of one's lusts and lowering people to sex object status. It can become entangled with the obsessive compulsion of pornography and lead to increasingly perverse fantasies and desires — and possibly aggression against the opposite sex.[5]

The apostle Paul says you are not to be in that kind of bondage: "All things are lawful for me, but not all things are profitable. All things are lawful for me, but I will not be mastered by anything" (1 Corinthians 6:12). Don't let masturbation control you.

It is second-rate sex. What is the purpose of sex? For two people to become one, to experience intimacy, in marriage. Behind the very drive that causes you to masturbate is a deep desire to know and be known, to love and be loved. Masturbation is an attempt to experience what is meant for marriage outside of marriage. Masturbation is a substitute for the real thing. "Marriage should be honored by all, and the marriage bed kept pure, for God will judge the adulterer and all the sexually immoral" (Hebrews 13:4). Don't settle for second-rate sex.

Masturbation is not acceptable for you. Period. Walter and Ingrid Trobisch echo that conclusion when they address the issue of masturbation and personal defeat: "Usually deep down there is a feeling of dissatisfaction with oneself and with one's life, which one tries to overcome in a short moment of pleasure."[6] God wants to get you out of masturbation.

YOU CAN DEFEAT IT!

Through the Lord Jesus Christ you can walk away from masturbation. You no longer need to experience frustration, discouragement and condemnation. These steps will take the pressure off.

Get honest with God. Realize that the lustful thoughts that lead you to masturbation are a sin against God, even more than a sin against yourself. When you sin, you hurt God. In Psalm 51:4, David said it like this: "Against Thee, Thee only, have I sinned" (NASB). Get before God and confess your sin and guilt. The Bible promises that because of Jesus' death on the cross for your sins, you become clean: "If we confess our sins, he is faithful and just to forgive us our sins, and to cleanse us from all unrighteousness" (1 John 1:9, KJV). You are forgiven — clean. And every time you mess up in the future, come immediately to God, be honest about your sin and ask for cleansing.

Nail down a stake. A "stake" is a fixed point that marks the start of a journey. You must decide *now* that you are going to win this battle. Even though you will make some mistakes in the future, you will win — no matter what. Determine that you want to please God more than you want to satisfy yourself. Decide that you want victory and you won't stop, no matter how hard the struggle, until you have it. You must make the decision to "walk by the Spirit, and you will not carry out the desire of the flesh" (Galatians 5:16, NASB). Make that decision *now*.

Plug into power. Recognize that you cannot win this battle in your own power. Only Jesus Christ living in you can change your desires and habits. "No, in all these things we are more than conquerors through him who loved us" (Romans 8:37). This promise is true for you in this situation. The best way to build up His strength in you is to *pray*. Begin now to have a regular, consistent time with the Lord every day for at least fifteen minutes. When you pray, commit your mind and body to Him, asking Him to "strengthen you with power through his Spirit in your inner being" (Ephesians 3:16). (Note: You can order the book *Spending Time Alone With God* from Reach Out Ministries to help you plan your time with God.)

Renew your mind. This problem started in your mind, so let God change your mind. Paul tells us, "Do not be conformed to this world, but be transformed by the renewing of your mind . . ." (Romans 12:2, NASB). God's way of renewing your mind is to get you into the Bible. That's where God's thoughts are found. He wants His thoughts to become your thoughts. Then any time you have a lustful thought you can immediately counter it by turning to God's thoughts. Jeremiah 15:16 challenges you: "When your words came, I ate them; they were my joy and my heart's delight, for I bear your name, O LORD God Almighty."

You need to devour God's words in the Bible every day. Set aside a time to read one chapter of the Bible every day for one month.   Let it soak in by memorizing a verse every week.   (Start with the list in chapter 7.)   Make a decision *now* to renew your mind with God's Word every day.

Focus your eyes.   Keep your eyes away from anything that turns you on sexually.   Obviously you can't live in a monastery, so your eyes *will* see sexually stimulating objects.   But *don't keep on looking at them* — especially pornographic material, soap operas or R-rated movies.   Jesus says this is important because "the eye is the lamp of the body. If your eyes are good, your whole body will be full of light. But if your eyes are bad, your whole body will be full of darkness" (Matthew 6:22,23).

Job, in the Old Testament, had a great idea for focusing his eyes.   He said, "I made a covenant with my eyes not to look lustfully at a girl" (Job 31:1).   Right *now* make a covenant with your eyes.   Commit yourself that you will focus your eyes on Jesus anytime you are sexually stimulated. That commitment will not only change the focus of your eyes, but also neutralize your body.

Control your body.   When your body feels like it will explode if some of the sexual pressure isn't let off, what do you do?   You bring it under control!   Paul tells us in 1 Corinthians 9:27: "No, I beat my body and make it my slave, so that after I have preached to others, I myself will not be disqualified for the prize."   Here are some ways you can "beat" your body.

- Exercise — Regular, consistent exercise burns off that excess energy.   Work out until all of the tension is gone.
- Help others — When you do something for someone else, that takes the focus off of yourself and your sexual tensions.   Look for ways to help others spiritually, because helping them to overcome their problems puts your focus on God and that person.
- Have fun — Get involved in creative, fun activities with your friends.   When your body tension rises,

call a friend and do something together.

Confide in a friend. When you share this problem with someone else, it provides the extra motivation you need to deal with it. Look for someone of the same sex who is spiritually mature and can help you. Ask that person to keep it confidential and to hold you accountable. Get him or her to ask you regularly if you are avoiding lust. Ecclesiastes 4:9,10 says, "Two are better than one, because they have a good return for their work: If one falls down, his friend can help him up. But pity the man who falls and has no one to help him up!" Decide *now* who that friend will be and talk with him or her today.

Avoid tempting situations. You can easily get drawn into sexually stimulating situations every day. All you have to do is live. How do you deal with it? Paul says, "Put on the Lord Jesus Christ, and make no provision for the flesh in regard to its lusts" (Romans 13:14, NASB). First, put on the Lord Jesus. Do that every morning as you dress. Put Him on like you put on your clothes. He will go with you all day and protect you.

Second, make no provision for your flesh. You can do that by resisting the second look at a sensually dressed person, and avoiding magazines and TV shows that stimulate you sexually (be careful of cable). Be on guard when you're alone, especially where it's easy to be tempted: in the bathroom, in the shower, at bedtime. Don't hang around in the bed in the morning. Guard against fantasizing about past sensual encounters. Stay clear of conversations with others about sex. *Decide now* to take Paul's words seriously: "But among you there must not even be a hint of sexual immorality, or of any kind of impurity" (Ephesians 5:3).

Press on despite failure. If you fail, don't get discouraged. It took time to get into this habit, it will take time to get out of it. Don't hang around condemning and hating yourself. Failure may happen, but it's not final. Most people don't stop immediately and never do it again. If you fall, don't lie in the dirt, but get up and dust yourself off. Do that by immediately confessing your sins and by receiving

God's forgiveness in faith. Don't worry about how many times you ask forgiveness.[7] Jesus has forgiven you, and He will keep on doing that "seventy times seven" (Matthew 18:22).

Don't, though, accept failure easily. It's *always* a choice when you sin, and God wants you not to sin. First Corinthians 10:13 tells you, "No temptation has seized you except what is common to man. And God is faithful; he will not let you be tempted beyond what you can bear. But when you are tempted, he will also provide a way out so that you can stand up under it." Take the way of escape.

Go for total victory. "Is that possible?" you ask. You bet.

You are free. You don't have to sin. You don't have to let the radiator get overheated. And if it does, you have the cross of Christ to make you clean again and His resurrection power to get control again. Let these words challenge you to freedom and obedience:

> In the same way, count yourselves dead to sin but alive to God in Christ Jesus. Therefore do not let sin reign in your mortal body so that you obey its evil desires. Do not offer the parts of your body to sin, as instruments of wickedness, but rather offer yourselves to God, as those who have been brought from death to life; and offer the parts of your body to him as instruments of righteousness. For sin shall not be your master, because you are not under law, but under grace (Romans 6:11-14).

When you walk in that freedom and obedience, just think of all the energy you will have as a powerful man or woman of God. That sexual energy will be channeled to make an impact for Jesus Christ through your life!

With the power of Jesus Christ in you, defeating masturbation is definitely possible. Thousands of Christians are testimony to that fact. Praise the Lord — He can do it in you, too. Don't quit until He does. Here is His promise that we want to pass on to you: "So do not fear, for I am with you; do not be dismayed, for I am your God. I will strengthen you and help you; I will uphold you with my righteous right hand" (Isaiah 41:10).

     Trust Christ.

     Obey Him.

     He will give you total victory!

ACTION SECTION

     1. Write a paragraph on why you are convinced masturbation is wrong for you.

_____

_____

_____

_____

_____

     2. Walk through each of the steps. Write down the decisions you make and how Jesus will defeat masturbation in you.

My decision	My progress
Record your decisions below.	Jot a note when you take a step.

A.   Get honest with God.

     My confession about masturbation:

_____   _____

_____   _____

_____   _____

B.   Nail down a stake.

     My decision to win over masturbation:

_____   _____

_____   _____

_____   _____

C. Plug into power.

My fifteen minutes with God is at ———— A.M./P.M. every day for thirty days. Check when you do this each day.

____ ____ ____ ____ ____ ____ ____ ____ ____ ____

____ ____ ____ ____ ____ ____ ____ ____ ____ ____

____ ____ ____ ____ ____ ____ ____ ____ ____ ____

D. Renew your mind.

The book of the Bible I will read this month is

————————. The verses I will memorize this month:

(1) _____

(2) _____

(3) _____

(4) _____

E. Focus your eyes.

My eyes will *not* focus on:

My eyes *will* focus on:

F. Control your body.

My exercise program:

My plan to help others:

My plan to have fun:

G. Confide in a friend.
      My friend who will hold me accountable:
_____ Check   here   when   you   have
talked to your friend. _____

H. Avoid tempting situations.
      Tempting situations I will avoid:
(1) _____
(2) _____
(3) _____

I. Allow for failure.
      My prayer asking forgiveness when I mess up:

_____
_____
_____

J. Go for total victory.
      The promise of victory: "So do not fear, for I am
with you; do not be dismayed, for I am your God. I will
strengthen you and help you; I will uphold you with my
righteous right hand" (Isaiah 41:10).

9

We're Pregnant — What Do We Do? ♥

*J*im came to talk to us in a panic — a few days earlier, tests had confirmed that his girlfriend was pregnant. We had known both Jim and Susan for several months. Here is how he explained what happened:

> At first we were friends, enjoying long, intense conversations. The interest grew into dating. But when kissing got out of hand, we broke up, remaining friends. I was determined not to let my body get ahead of my emotions. I was not in love with her.
>
> We didn't see each other that summer, but when we returned to school in the fall we were charged with emotional excitement for one another. We spent hours together every day. We were in love, and we began doing more and more physically. After having sex, we knew it was wrong. After a few times, we stopped. That's why her words hit so hard three weeks later — "I think I'm pregnant."

That night we walked for miles, as if by walking long enough, fast enough, we could escape this problem. How could we walk out from under this ugly cloud that was hanging over us?

The test confirmed it. We were pregnant.

Turmoil flooded my emotions. *God, why do You hate me? Why are You trying to ruin my life?* I felt like a disgrace, worth nothing to anyone, without any future, a scum.

After wrestling with the problem every minute for a week, I finally faced talking to my parents.

The news broke my parents' hearts. My father was silent; my mother started lecturing. I walked out.

When we talked again, my father said they loved me. He was crying. My mother tried to console me with deep sympathy, but I couldn't bear what I had done to my father.

I tore up my room — ripping, breaking, kicking and throwing everything violently. I leaned out the window. If I did a head-first dive into that car below, that would end it. I'd die for certain. Then maybe I'd stop being such a disgrace, a loser, a shame to my family.

Then I just collapsed and cried.

Pregnancy happens to hundreds of thousands of teenagers every year. Chances are great that one of your friends is in that situation right now. Or maybe you are yourself.

Panic is your first reaction. In a pregnancy situation, it is impossible to see clearly on your own. People wear glasses to get their vision corrected. Here are the "glasses" that will help you look at the problem realistically and choose the best action.

ACCEPT GOD'S LOVE AND FORGIVENESS

Everything inside of you screams out, "What a fool!" Your feelings about yourself and your sex partner are intense. Your emotions are going through a cycle something like this:

Disbelief: "We're not really pregnant. It's just an illusion, or something."

Escape: "We'll get an abortion, or run away. I'll kill myself."

Guilt: "I feel so dirty. I'm guilty."

Anger and self-hatred: "I hate myself. I'll never forgive myself."

Bitterness: "I hate him." "I'll never forgive her."

Confrontation: "We're pregnant. It's true. We accept that and we'll deal with it God's way."

In the middle of all of these emotions, remember that Jesus loves you and He accepts you. He does not condemn you. But everything inside of you says, "No way. He hates me. He doesn't want to have anything to do with me."

Consider how Jesus treated a woman in a similar situation — read John 8:3-11 right now.

You have a decision to make. You got into this by a self-centered, short-sighted choice. Now God wants you to make another choice — to receive His love and forgiveness. You probably feel like Jim: "God must hate me. God is punishing me. I'm not worth God's love." This is a hard step, but it's one you need to take. Don't go on until you honestly, openly pray this prayer. Read it aloud, then pray it to God:

Lord Jesus, I know I have sinned against myself, and others, but most of all I have sinned against You. I confess that sin now. Lord, I had sex and created life outside of Your plan for me. That was wrong. I'm guilty. Right now I accept the fact that You love me so much that You died for my sin. I receive Your love and forgiveness. Thank You, Lord, that You do not condemn me, but that You accept me.

Praying that prayer changes the way you see everything. Now, instead of being alone and condemned, you are loved and accepted. That love will heal you. (For a more in-depth discussion of God's love and forgiveness, see chapter 11.)

TAKE RESPONSIBILITY FOR THE PAST

Once the initial shock has worn off, you need to take a serious look at why this happened. Only when you accept responsibility can you turn to God for the strength to handle it. You will experience healing and change in your life. God can then use this experience to accomplish His purpose in your life — conforming you to the likeness of His Son, Jesus Christ (Romans 8:28,29).

Guys, Why Did You Get Her Pregnant?

Some guys feel like this: "She's carrying the baby. It's her problem." That is ridiculous. This pregnancy is no less a problem for you than it is for her.

Let this sink in: *You are responsible!* You got her pregnant.

Probably it happened something like this: "When I asked her out, everything was fine. I really enjoyed her company, but I wanted more. We got physically involved, and she tried to stop me. We promised each other that we wouldn't do that anymore. But I pressured her. She liked me and didn't want to disappoint me, so she gave in. We had sex. I didn't even think she would get pregnant."

Notice what you are responsible for:

- *Selfishness* — "I wanted more."
- *Lust* — "We got physically involved."
- *Lying* — "We promised . . ." (You didn't mean it.)
- *Disrespect* — "I pressured her."
- *Impurity* — "We had sex."
- *Irresponsibility* — "I didn't even think . . ."

Come before God and ask Him to give you the courage to accept the responsibility for your actions. Ask Him to forgive you. Then respond correctly by obeying God. Follow the advice in chapters 11 and 12 to know how to respond with obedience.

Girls, Why Did You Get Pregnant?

Every girl has different reasons. Whatever your reasons, you must accept responsibility for your actions. You decide which reasons brought you to this place.

Pressure. This pressure comes either from your girl-friends or your boyfriend. You didn't say no.

Fulfillment. Often girls feel that having a baby will make them feel fulfilled as a woman. You may have been lonely, and you may have thought, *I'll have a baby who I can love and who will love me back.* When you have the baby, reality will set in. That desire for love gets covered up by dirty diapers. It's unrealistic to expect that an infant can give, or even receive, the love you're looking for.

Independence. Others believe pregnancy will result in maturity and independence. You can quit school (eight out of ten girls do), get out on your own and have a regular source of income (welfare). You may think that having a baby means you can be your own boss.[1] How shocking to discover that you are now more dependent on others than ever before.

Expectations. False expectations lead many girls into sexual intercourse. Your reasoning may have been: "I thought he wouldn't like me if I didn't," or "I thought being pregnant would make him marry me."[2]

Identify the reasons you got pregnant. Confess those reasons to God. Tell Him that you are responsible. Ask Him to dig down deep into your life and heal your attitudes and emotions.

For Both of You

Your action carries responsibility. Your action affects you, your partner, the baby, your parents, your partner's parents, people at church, friends at school and those you influence.

What you need to do now is to accept that responsibility. But the burden is too heavy; you can't carry it on your own. *You need Jesus to shoulder the burden of responsibility.* The Bible promises: "Cast all your anxiety on him because he cares for you" (1 Peter 5:7). With Jesus you can make it! Jesus will take your burdens on Himself and take you through this difficult time.

GET HELP

You don't need to go through this alone. In fact, you can't. People have to know. Here are the steps to follow to get a support system around you.

Go immediately to someone you trust. If you have had a good relationship with your parents, go first to them. If not, make sure the person you confide in is an older adult (your pastor, youth minister, Sunday school teacher, a Christian couple) who will listen and be able to advise you wisely.

Go together. With your counselor, talk to your boyfriend/the father or girlfriend/the mother. The involvement of the father of the child is crucial at this point — you are in this together. You need to solve the problem together. Both of you need to take responsibility for your actions.

Tell your counselor everything. You may want to "save face" by giving reasons and excuses. Instead, be honest about what happened. Tell your counselor:

- how you got pregnant;
- when it happened;
- how long you have been having intercourse;
- how you feel — your fears, disappointments, regrets and guilt;
- how you prayed the prayer on page 129.

Tell your parents. Of all the trials you face, this may be the hardest, but you're dealing with reality, so you *must* talk to them — not weeks later, but *now.*

Ask your counselor to set up the meeting with both sets of parents and to be present when you tell them. Ask him or her to help you write down what you need to say to your parents so you can express it correctly. Remember, you have no control over your parents' response. Their response may be one of these:

- Confusion — "Where did we go wrong?"
- Hurt — "How could you do this to us?"
- Hatred — "We don't want you to ever set foot in this house again."

- Anger at the girl — "You filthy tramp."
- Anger at the boy — "We hate you."
- Compassion and love — "We accept you and want to help."

Be prepared for the initial shock. But whatever their first emotional response, they will calm down as time goes by.

Both sets of parents will probably want to get together to discuss the situation. Ask your counselor to handle that meeting so positive results will follow.

All of these steps are very painful, but necessary. You will want to run and hide. But face each situation honestly and directly. God will honor that.

MAKE NECESSARY DECISIONS

Once you have talked with your parents, some serious decisions need to be made. Make the best decisions possible. Have your counselor check into a Christian pregnancy counseling center in your area. The center will be able to help you with decisions like:

- Options: Should you marry or not marry? Should you put the baby up for adoption or keep it?
- Doctor: Which doctor will you go to?
- Finances: How will you pay for the doctor? For the baby? The center will help you apply for Medicaid to cover financial costs.
- Housing: Where will you live? They'll help you decide if it's better to stay at home or to go to a home for pregnant girls.
- Diet: The center will help you know how to eat properly in order to nourish the baby.

EXAMINE YOUR OPTIONS

Let's get a clear picture of the options available to you at this point.

Guys

You are asking, what do I do now? You're probably confused and bewildered. What can you do?

Take charge. Take responsibility for the decisions that need to be made. Make a list of the steps of action that you and she will need to take, and check them off as you complete them.

When appropriate, offer marriage. Although you must take responsibility for the baby, you do not need to marry your girlfriend. Offer marriage only if you are convinced that this is the right person for you for life. If both sets of parents give approval, and you both are emotionally stable, spiritually giving, and physically and financially able to exist apart from your parents, offer marriage.

Take care of the child. You need to take financial responsibility for the girl to have the baby. All of this can be done at a minimal cost through the pregnancy counseling center. You may not have the money, so that means you'll need to go to your parents for a loan (with the provision that you'll pay them back in nine months). Get a job in the meantime, save your money and start learning sound financial principles.[3]

Girls

You're asking, what do I do now? And you're asking urgently, because you're carrying the baby. What approach do you need to take?

Don't do anything rash. You will tend to panic. Instead, look to the Lord and keep calm. If you have thoughts of committing suicide, running away, getting married secretly or having an abortion, don't follow through with them. You need time to think all the way through the situation with the advice of older counselors.

Consult with others. You will tend to try to handle this on your own. But you need the help of others to make the right decisions.

Make a decision. The final decision about the baby

is yours. You will have to live with this decision the rest of your life.

Let's examine the options open to you and your boy-friend/girlfriend.

Option One: Abortion

As a Christian, you can't even consider abortion as an option.

> After my abortion, I was so filled with regret, re-morse, and self-hate that I became anorexic and nearly starved myself to death. I spent thirty-two weeks in the psychiatric unit of a hospital where I had a series of shock treatments and escaped the pain by prescription drugs. I not only abused drugs and alcohol, but I attempted suicide twice.

That girl isn't alone. According to the most recent statistics, over 1.5 million abortions are performed in the USA each year.

Why is this not for you?

You abort life. Medical science confirms that life begins at conception, not birth.[4] The Bible teaches the value of human life — even in the womb. Jacob and Esau had a fight in their mother's womb (Genesis 25:21-24). David claimed God was his God from his mother's womb (Psalm 22:9,10). Jeremiah's destiny was determined from his mother's womb (Jeremiah 1:4,5). John the Baptist responded in his mother's womb to the news of Jesus (Luke 1:41).

God is actively involved in the life of an unborn child. Psalm 139:13-16 says:

> For you created my inmost being; you knit me to-gether in my mother's womb. I praise you because I am fearfully and wonderfully made; your works are wonderful, I know that full well. My frame was not hidden from you when I was made in the secret place. When I was woven together in the depths of the earth, your eyes saw my un-formed body. All the days ordained for me were written in

your book before one of them came to be.

To have an abortion is to murder another human
being. God said in Exodus 20:13, "You shall not murder."
You have already made one mistake. To kill your baby
would add a tragedy on top of a mistake.

You abort health. Abortion often causes damage to
the reproductive organs. Heavy loss of blood, risk of infec-
tion and puncturing of the uterus add up to damaged health.
Abortion can lead to future pregnancy problems as well —
premature birth, misplaced pregnancy (the baby develops in
the fallopian tube or cervix, not the uterus), miscarriage and
birth complications. Abortion may cause infertility (the inabil-
ity to become pregnant again).[5]

You abort emotions. Even though abortion seems to
be the easy way out, in the long run you will burden yourself
with guilt, depression and anxiety. These feelings will make
it impossible to ever forget the abortion.[6]

You abort responsibility. You chose to have sex and
the result is a baby. Now you have an opportunity to learn
real responsibility. Abortion is an escape from that responsibility. It prevents you from going through the hard but valuable learning experience of dealing with the consequences of
your actions. This is your opportunity to grow up. Don't
miss it.

You abort self-respect. That doesn't seem right. It
would seem that if you get an abortion, people would not
know about the pregnancy and you would keep your self-
respect. Not so. Respect is what others think of you, but
self-respect is what you think about yourself. Even if nobody
else knows, an abortion damages your self-respect, making
you feel like a murderer. Keep your self-respect.

You abort social responsibility. Our society has ad-
vocated the murder of babies and blown it off as no big deal.
"Most medical researchers believe it is only a matter of time
before fetal tissue [aborted babies] is routinely used." Babies' brains and livers are used to treat diseases with no
thought to the killed baby. Since the organs need to be taken

from the babies as quickly as possible, some may be removed while the baby is still alive.[7]

You don't want to be a part of this. Abortion is not the easy way out. Your baby is already a human being.

Abortion is *not* an option.

Option Two: Marriage

If an unmarried couple discover they're pregnant, will marriage make it right? *Absolutely not!* Even though marriage is not morally wrong, it has built-in problems.

Marriage takes maturity. Most teenagers think of themselves as mature, but in reality they have a lot of growing up to do. Dr. Ed Wheat in his book, *Intended for Pleasure,* says immature teenage marriages tend to fail. Why? First, teenagers, in most cases, cannot separate from their parents and become independent. Second, teenagers have changing value systems. They don't really know yet what they want in a mate. Personality traits which were not apparent at the time the young people were married will surface later; a person's character develops as a response to responsibility or adversity. There is no way to predict with accuracy how a teenager will respond to the difficulties and demands of married life in the years ahead.[8]

Marriage complicates the relationship. If you choose a hurried wedding, the chances are great that it will end in divorce. If your partner is immature and not ready for parenthood, then it will lead only to tension, frustration and fighting. If either one of you marries unwillingly, the marriage won't stand the pressure.

Marriage is built on love, not selfishness. When two people enter a marriage filled-up emotionally — having received love and having confidence and security — then they are ready for marriage. Otherwise you will approach the relationship selfishly. Two empty, insecure people don't have much to give. Even one full glass can't fill up an empty one without running out itself. It takes a lot of love — "give and take" and "give and give" — for a marriage to work and for a couple to be able to raise children.[9]

Marriage is holy. The Bible says "Marriage should be honored by all, and the marriage bed kept pure" (Hebrews 13:4). Because your relationship has not been pure, it is difficult to enter into holy marriage. Jesus Christ can make you pure (see chapter 11). But before marriage is an option, you must work through becoming pure yourself. Otherwise you will battle guilt in your marriage.

This option is for you *only if* both of you are mature, *if* both of you want marriage and parenthood, *if* your relationship is built on love and not selfishness, and *if* you can have a holy, guilt-free marriage.

Only *if* you can honestly fulfill these requirements should you consider marriage an option.

Option Three: Single Parenting

This option means the mother decides to give birth to the baby and keep it without getting married, or the father takes the child after birth. Consider this option carefully. Let's look at the advantages and disadvantages.[10]

Advantages

- You can live at home and get your family's help in raising your child. Trying to live on your own, with a job and a new baby, is almost impossible. Let your family help.
- Your child has an established home.
- You don't have to enter into a quick and undesirable marriage.
- You can more easily carry on your schooling and friendships.
- You have readily available emotional and financial support, as well as a wealth of parenting experience from your parents.

Disadvantages

- You might have problems with your parents, particularly your mother. You will have more than

two people raising the child and conflicts are certain to occur.
- Your concept of motherhood or fatherhood is probably very naive. This is not playing dolls. Raising an infant and toddler is very hard work, with very little sleep and tremendous demands on your time and energy.
- You may let the raising of the child fall back to your mother. You and your mom need very good, clear communication on what is expected.

Depending on how you fit into the advantages and disadvantages, single parenting may or may not be for you.

Option Four: Adoption

Adoption means that you give birth to the baby, then let another family adopt him or her. Let's look at the advantages and disadvantages.

Advantages

- You can be responsible to your unborn baby without locking yourself, your boyfriend/girlfriend, and your parents into a life-long commitment.
- You can know that your baby will benefit from the love and support that a married couple can give.[11] These parents have been longing for a child and are eager to love and care for the baby.
- You can know that your baby will be placed according to your desires. Adoption agencies have high standards that adoption couples must meet. The agency does their best to place your baby in a home that meets your requirements in ethnic background, religion, educational level and other areas important to you.
- You can have the adoptive parents pay the medical expenses involved.[12]

Disadvantages

- You will experience deep pain. After you've been through a nine-month pregnancy with your baby, he or she will be hard to give up.
- You will grieve. This will be the end of the most intimate of all human relationships. If you feel strongly, insist that you see your baby after birth. This may help ease your grief.

Depending on your situation, adoption could be a good option for you.

THE FINAL DECISION IS YOURS

After receiving counsel from parents, your boyfriend or girlfriend, and your counselor, the two of you have to make a decision. Make it together. Live it out together. Both of you must live with the consequences of your choice, so the final decision is yours. No one can force a decision on you — you must make it yourself. Seek God's will at every step. As you do, God will work Romans 8:28 in your life: "And we know that in all things God works for the good of those who love him, who have been called according to his purpose."

ACTION SECTION

If, girls, you have gotten pregnant, or, guys, you have gotten your girlfriend pregnant, read and follow each step. If you are reading this to counsel another person now, or in the future, write down the steps you will take to help them.

1. After praying the prayer on page 129, describe how you have received God's love and forgiveness.

_____

_____

_____

2. Guys, why did you get her pregnant?   Girls, why did you get pregnant?

_____

_____

_____

3. Who is your main counselor?   _____
Where and when will you meet him or her?

_____

_____

_____

4. Girls, what will you tell your boyfriend? Boys, what will you tell your girlfriend?

_____

_____

_____

5. When and where will you talk to your parents?

_____

What will you say?

_____

_____

_____

6. Where are you going for pregnancy counseling? (Your parents should be able to help with this.) Have you confirmed that it is a Christian organization? (Don't visit it before you have.)

_____

Write down what the counseling center advises you to do:

_____

_____

_____

_____

7. Review the advice you listed in question 6 with your parents and counselor. Write down the option you will choose — besides abortion — and the steps you will need to take.

Option: _____

_____

Doctor: _____

_____

Finances: _____

_____

Housing: _____

_____

Diet: _____

_____

Other: _____

_____

10

How Do I Handle Sexual Problems? ♥

*S*ex is powerful. When misused or abused, sex can seriously wound you. Like playing around with a loaded pistol, there's potential for destroying yourself.

Sex wounded one young man we know like that. Abused during childhood, he grew up emotionally wounded, even though he knew Jesus Christ. Because he was wounded, he expressed his sexuality incorrectly — through homosexual activity. That wounded him even more. Today he says: "Because I was wounded in childhood, I was crippled in my emotional and physical responses as an adult." These problems haunted him so much that at one point he took out a gun to commit suicide. He was desperate.

Jesus is the Healer of wounds — spiritual, physical and emotional. He said, "It is not the healthy who need a doctor, but the sick. I have not come to call the righteous, but sinners to repentance" (Luke 5:31,32). When our friend turned to God, Jesus healed him. In fact, Jesus has done such a great work of healing that our friend is completely well emotionally and is serving God as an overseas missionary.

Jesus will do the same for you if you are experiencing sexual problems. Whatever you do, don't give up and give in to your problems. Instead, face them head on.

This chapter covers the most common sexual problems that wound students. The first part looks at problems that you create. The second part deals with ones in which you are the victim. There's not enough space to cover each one thoroughly in one chapter, but each section will help you identify the wounds and give you some practical help to begin the healing process.

When you're the cause . . .

PORNOGRAPHY

Many students, guys and girls, are into pornography, whether it's the sexy picture hanging on your wall or the magazines stacked under your mattress. In fact, in one survey 99 percent of the young men and 91 percent of the young women had read or looked at pornographic books or magazines.[1]

One look doesn't make you a sexual weirdo, but psychologists say that continuing such activity can lead to severe problems. For example, seven teenage boys attacked a fifteen-year-old girl. Four of them admitted that pornography incited their attack. In another instance, a thirteen-year-old boy attacked a young girl. He was stimulated by a sex magazine article, "How to Strip a Woman."

Pornography treats men and women as sex objects. It cheapens sex. Even more, it gets a stronghold on your mind and controls your thoughts. You are drawn to pornography any time you become lonely or sexually stimulated. At some point, you cross an invisible line — you begin to put into practice physically what you have been imagining mentally. You move from lust to immorality. You find yourself in a vicious, out-of-control cycle that eventually takes over your life.

To combat this problem (which probably includes masturbation as well), study chapters 7, 8 and 12 and take every necessary action for deliverance.

ORAL SEX

Oral sex is defined as stimulating the partner's genitals with the tongue or mouth. This is done in order to have an orgasm without having intercourse. People who are involved with oral sex often want to remain "technical virgins," but they're still involved in sexual immorality. Somehow they miss Jesus' whole idea: "Marriage should be honored by all, and the marriage bed kept pure" (Hebrews 13:4). God created sex for communication and oneness inside of the marriage commitment. When a person is involved in oral sex outside of marriage, the marriage bed is defiled.

Oral sex is one step short of intercourse. For you to justify doing it by saying, "I haven't gone all the way," is not good enough in God's eyes. He wants you to be free not only of immorality, but also impurity (see Ephesians 5:3).

If this is a problem for you, study chapters 5 and 12 and take every step to restore sexual purity to your life.

SEXUALLY TRANSMITTED DISEASES

One of the great tragedies of our day is sexually transmitted diseases. These diseases are a direct result of ignoring God's provision and protection by having random sex, often before marriage.

Sexually transmitted diseases will be the most significant health problem for the rest of the twentieth century. For example, *Newsweek* says, "This year more babies will be affected by sexually transmitted diseases than were affected by polio during the entire polio epidemic of the '50s."[2] These diseases are at epidemic proportions. If you have been involved in illicit sexual activity, or homosexual activity, then your health and life can be tragically affected by these diseases. If not, then you need to know how to help others in this difficult situation.

A sexually transmitted disease (STD) is passed along from one person to another by intercourse or oral sex. Contrary to rumor, these diseases have not been shown to be transmitted through toilet seats, dirty towels, food, water or unsanitary objects.

New strains are discovered every year. Here are the most common.

Gonorrhea. Known as clap, morning drip or gleet, this bacteria affects the genital organs, joints, skin, mouth and arms. In men the symptoms are pain in urinating, and a discharge of pus. In women there are no external symptoms.

Syphilis. The syphilis bacteria dies in seconds away from the body, but in the body syphilis is deadly. Symptoms start out as open sores which disappear and recur. If left untreated, syphilis can lead to heart problems and brain damage.

Herpes. Herpes is a virus with no cure. It appears as cold sores on any part of the body. These sores can be external or internal, many or few, large or small, and can be triggered into multiplying rapidly. Some of the factors that trigger herpes are premenstrual tension, intercourse, emotional tension or fever. Worry about an attack can prompt new attacks.

AIDS (Acquired Immune Deficiency Syndrome). This is one of the most frightening diseases in history, and it's growing at epidemic proportions. Seventy-three percent of the people who get AIDS are homosexual men. The other 27 percent are intravenous drug users, recipients of blood transfusions, hemophiliacs and those who have heterosexual relationships with AIDS victims or carriers. The disease is transmitted through the blood or semen. It affects the body's natural ability to prevent disease. Symptoms are similar to those of the flu — chronic cough, weight loss, diarrhea, fatigue. No one is cured and no one recovers from AIDS — all eventually die[3]

If you have one of these diseases, or know someone

who does, you need to talk to someone: your parents, your youth minister, your pastor or a counselor. Get to a doctor as quickly as you can. To keep it a secret will only make matters worse.

If you want to keep from having these diseases, the solution is very simple — don't get involved in premarital sex. The Bible is right: "This is the will of God . . . that you abstain from sexual immorality" (1 Thessalonians 4:3, NASB).

HOMOSEXUALITY

Most teenagers, in the process of finding their own sexual identity, have homosexual thoughts and fantasies. Therefore, many students worry about whether or not they are gay. The fear of homosexuality is common among teenagers. Adolescence is a time when you experience new and intense sexual feelings and sexual interest. Perhaps someone labeled you "gay" because you are a tomboy, or you don't fit the macho image, or you have a close friend of the same sex.

To put your mind at ease, none of these things make you a homosexual.

A homosexual is a person who is unusually attracted to, and finds sexual satisfaction with, someone of the same sex. If you find yourself in that category, then read this section carefully to discover how you got into homosexuality and how you can get out. The only two real requirements are (1) you want to get out of homosexuality, and (2) you will trust Jesus to work in you.

The Causes. Although no genetic sources for homosexual behavior have been determined (despite much research), homosexuality can be caused by several known environmental factors:

1. An overprotective mother and an absent or uninvolved father. An unloving or cruel father also can cause a boy to turn to homosexuality. We have yet to meet someone with homosexual behavior who had a strong, loving father.

2. An exposure, while growing up, to boys and girls

who either tempted you or forced you into homosexual stimulation and practice. This happens often with an older brother,
sister or a neighbor.

3. Viewing homosexual pornographic movies or
magazines or actual homosexual behavior can act as a temptation to experiment with homosexual behavior[4]

The Solution. If this is a problem for you, turn to the
Bible to find God's solution. You must believe that what
God says about you is true!

- A person with homosexual behavior who has received Christ has a new personality. He (or she)
  has the power to live like God intended him to
  live (see 2 Corinthians 5:17). A Christian has a
  new capacity to handle this problem and to make
  right choices.

- Homosexual behavior violates God's pattern of
  sexual expression. Romans 1:27 says, "In the
  same way the men also abandoned natural relations
  with women and were inflamed with lust for one
  another. Men committed indecent acts with other
  men, and received in themselves the due penalty
  for their perversion." Homosexuality violates the
  very nature of our bodies.

- Homosexual behavior is not an unpardonable sin.
  It is a sin no better or worse than any other sin
  that keeps you from being all God created you to
  be. In 1 Corinthians 6:9-11, Paul says:

> Do you not know that the wicked will not inherit the
> kingdom of God? Do not be deceived: Neither the sexually
> immoral nor idolaters nor adulterers nor male prostitutes nor
> homosexual offenders nor thieves nor the greedy nor drunkards
> nor slanderers nor swindlers will inherit the kingdom of God.
> And that is what some of you *were.* But you were *washed*
> [all your sins cleaned away], you were *sanctified* [set apart for
> God to use], you were *justified* [considered sinless before God]
> in the name of the Lord Jesus Christ and by the Spirit of our
> God.

Sanctified means separated *from* all the habits and associations of homosexuality and separated *to* Jesus for Him to do whatever He wants with your life at whatever the cost.[5]

God wants to end homosexual behavior and to heal homosexuals. He wants to bring you and every other person to fullness in Christ. We personally have counseled numerous people who have been set free from the bondage of homosexuality. The best way for that to happen is for you to get involved with an organization designed specifically to help you. Contact EXODUS INTERNATIONAL, P. O. Box 2121, San Rafael, CA 99412. They can refer you to a Christian ministry in your area.

When you're the victim . . .

SEXUAL ABUSE

Sexual abuse is widespread. In fact, each year one out of ten American young people are abused.[6] One in four females and more than one in ten males remember being sexually abused before their eighteenth birthday.[7] Yet only 6 percent of the incidents are ever reported to authorities.[8] The odds are great that you, too, have been sexually abused.

Do you, or someone you know, identify with this experience?

For ten years of my childhood I was trapped in secrecy, tangled within a web of sexual abuse by my own father and others in my neighborhood. The secret was exposed when I was thirteen . . . I was so ashamed and afraid. I was afraid of how people would treat me if they knew the truth . . . I saw no way out . . . I thought I had committed the unpardonable sin.

Sexual abuse takes two primary forms: incest and teen prostitution.

Incest

Incest is having sexual relations with a member of

your own family. Two people too closely related by blood to be married engage in sexual activity. In your family there *should* be expressions of physical affection. But when expressions of affection become sexual, they are incestuous. There is no such thing as a positive experience involving incest.

The most common relationship where sexual abuse occurs is between father and daughter. Usually the father has an excessive need to be with his daughter and have her do things for him (haircuts, massages, etc). At first, the daughter enjoys this because she feels special. But then sex play and intercourse are introduced by the father. His advances usually are not resisted by the daughter because she finds it pleasurable, or her father lies, telling her this is how people show love, or her father threatens her.

The daughter will have several emotional responses besides the pleasure of the sexual arousal, including fear, guilt and anger. Since she has been raised to obey and trust her parents, she is quite vulnerable to her father's seduction. Unfortunately she often blames herself for what's happening. Sometimes the mother, by intuition, knows what is going on, but she denies it. If this happens, the family secret remains a secret, making everything look OK on the outside in hopes of keeping the family from blowing apart.[9]

Other expressions of incestuous abuse occur between brother and sister, mother and son, father and son, brother and brother, sister and sister.

These incestuous relationships have severe consequences. If you are abused, or know someone who is, these are some of the warning signs that let you know you need help:

Socially. An abused person often reacts with rage toward others and rebels against other authorities (since they are forced to obey parental authority) by committing petty crimes, skipping school or running away. The abused person may display seductive behavior, become promiscuous, or masturbate excessively. Often the victim will isolate himself (or herself).

Physically. A person who's abused may exhibit anorexia, nausea, vomiting, headaches, dizziness and fainting, constant infections, bruises or bleeding, and even self-destructive behavior such as drug or alcohol abuse.

Emotionally. He (or she) may appear hysterical, overly anxious or excessively depressed. The abused person often fears medical exams and may take an unusual number of baths. Other emotional signs include a fear and mistrust of others and low self-esteem.

Spiritually. The victim has difficulty accepting God's forgiveness, trusting God as Father, or obeying his (or her) parents. Often a judgmental attitude toward self and others is exhibited.

Teen Prostitution

An extreme expression of sexual abuse today is teen prostitution. Estimates of the number of teen prostitutes range from 100,000 to one million. Most teen prostitutes are runaways, and, contrary to popular belief, 80 percent are from white, middle- and upper-class families.[10]

Teen prostitution is closely tied in with pornography, because pedophiles (adults who seek sex with young children) publish as many as 260 child pornography magazines, using young people to pose for photographs in every imaginable sexual act. These people are drawn into this for drugs, alcohol and money. These pedophiles contact young people at school grounds, arcades, bus stations, malls and other places where you hang out. Be on your guard against suspicious adults in these situations.

Sexual abuse in both forms — incest and teen prostitution — is sick, disgusting, vile! If you have gotten pulled into it, *you can get out.* If you have not gotten involved, but you find yourself on the verge of it, realize that you are being victimized by another person, even though that person may be in your family. This is against God's plan for you. Leviticus 18:6 says, "No one is to approach any close relative to have sexual relations. I am the LORD." Read the rest of

Leviticus 18 to see how sexual abuse is against God's plan.

Don't blame yourself. Victims of sexual abuse often feel that the incident is their fault, producing unnecessary guilt and condemnation. You are not at fault and do not need to take the blame for another person's sickness. Instead, *take action* to stop the incestuous relationship — do not keep quiet about the problem. In order to do this, you'll need help. Talk to an adult with whom you have a close relationship (possibly your youth minister or pastor). Ask them to help you get professional guidance. You will need to talk to a qualified Christian counselor who can help you work through this and come out on the other side freed from it. If you do not have help locally, call one of these two organizations: For sexual abuse within your family, call the National Child Abuse Hotline, 1-800-422-4453; for sexual abuse outside your family, call the National Center for Missing and Exploited Children, 1-800-843-5678. There's no charge for the calls.

God wants to help you. One person, who, with the help of Jesus, had worked through being sexually abused, said, "He took my weakness and turned it into strength." He can do the same for you.

RAPE

Rape can happen to any woman, and it's happening more and more. What makes rape "rape"? Force. Force is used to penetrate a woman sexually without her consent. Rape happens in one of two ways.

Date Rape

Date rape is manipulating a person into sexual activities without her consent.

John ran into Susan after school. He walked her home. She looked really sexy. At her house he asked if he could come in. She said no because her parents weren't there. But he said, "Just for a drink of water." Once inside he forced himself on her.

Why does this happen? Because a guy wants to be
macho — he plays a power game. He gets what he wants at
a girl's expense. Unwritten rules tell guys that it's OK: Push
for sex. Make the move. Be tough. The girl might resist,
but she doesn't really want to.

This kind of rape happens between two people who
know each other, but it's still rape because force is used.

Violent Rape

Rape is most often inflicted not as a sexual crime, but
as a violent crime. Most rapists aren't so much interested in
sexual pleasure as they are in hurting and frightening their
victim.

To protect yourself from rape is better than to learn
to cope with it. Stay away from potentially dangerous situations by following these suggestions:

- Never hitchhike or pick up hitchhikers.
- Don't walk or jog alone at night.
- Carry a whistle or small blast horn.
- Don't get "picked up."
- Don't flirt.
- Don't invite someone into your house that you
  don't know.[11]

If you understand both the male rapist and the female
rape victim, you can understand even more about how to
protect yourself.

The rapist. Violent rapists share a similar background: lack of love, deep emotional needs, unstable childhood, weird ideas of women, sexual abuse. They are quite
immature, struggle with low self-esteem, have a distorted
view of sexuality and fail to accept responsibility for their
behavior. They are full of anger and hatred. When these
factors come together in a person, he acts out his aggression
by raping a woman.[12]

If you are like this, then you have some deep-seated
emotional problems. You need to get help. Tell someone
you trust that you want to get counseling, and ask that person

to help you find a qualified Christian counselor. This counseling will help you understand that Jesus Christ loves you, and He can and will change you and make you whole and healthy.

The rape victim. The emotional response of a raped woman depends on the intent of the rapist. If his intention is sexual release, then she will feel used. If his intent is hostility, then she will feel defenseless. If his intent is to overpower, then she will feel humiliated.

Her reactions will depend also on who raped her and the circumstances. Was the rapist a stranger? Lover? Relative? Was she gang raped? Did he threaten her? Use a weapon? Accuse her of wanting the sex? Betray her? The victim's reactions during and after the rape will be determined by what actually happened.[13]

What Do I Do?

When a woman is raped, whether it is date rape or violent rape, she experiences a great trauma. How can she respond?

During the rape. Deborah Roberts, in her book *Raped*, gives the following advice:

No one can tell you what course of action to take if you are attacked. Only you can decide that.

However, some rapes have been prevented by using different means of escape. Any one of these methods could work, but none are guaranteed:

1. Pray out loud.
2. Quote Scripture.
3. Scream (Don't scream "Help!" Scream "Fire!")
4. Fake a seizure.
5. Act crazy or mentally deranged.
6. Tell him it's the wrong time of the month.
7. Put an Alka-Seltzer tablet in your mouth (causes foaming at the mouth).
8. Urinate.
9. Force your finger down your throat to induce vomiting.

Trying to escape from him may not be as effective as inventing a way to make yourself repulsive, causing *him* to want to leave *you*.

Each situation is different, so try to remain calm and decide whether it's better to run, scream, fight back, talk, or submit . . .

Also, remember that an assailant does not usually wait around for the victim to dig in her purse for a weapon, and this weapon at best can only provide a brief moment for escape . . .

Most rapists expect a victim to be passive, so finding a way to throw him off guard momentarily may allow you to get away. But under no circumstances should you do anything to endanger your life, especially if the assailant has a weapon. Remember, rape is something you can get over. It is not worth [losing] your life [to try to escape].[14]

Immediately after the rape. Go immediately to a hospital or rape crisis center, and let a doctor check you and verify evidence of rape. Do not wash yourself before you go.

Most women feel a sense of relief that they're alive after a rape, but they also feel angry, humiliated, embarrassed, guilty and confused (often combined with physical sensations). Take your situation to the Lord in prayer, asking Him to make you feel accepted, guiltless and clean. Then find someone you can talk to, and express your feelings — get them all out.

The weeks and months after the rape. Talk to a Christian counselor, and continue to talk about the rape until you resolve it. As you work through it, don't blame yourself with thoughts like, *If I hadn't accepted the ride . . .* or *If I had tried harder to get away . . .* Remember, you didn't commit a crime — you were a victim.

Accept your virginity. If you were a virgin before the rape, God considers you a virgin now. *Medically*, your virginity is gone (the only requirement for losing your virginity medically is sexual penetration). Your lost virginity is a result of living in a world where sin invades everything and everyone *Spiritually*, though, God has a higher standard for virginity — a life of sexual purity. If you lived this lifestyle before the rape, you can continue to live it afterward. Spiritual virginity is a matter of choice. You had *no* choice in the rape. God knows your heart.

The problem now, though, is that you have to live with the emotional results of the rape. Jesus gives you the resources to overcome all the emotions you're going to struggle through. It's important for you to realize that you need to deal with your feelings directly, honestly and completely in order to prevent permanent emotional damage. For help in this process, you'll need a professional counselor.

Pray for emotional healing. We recommend you read David Seamand's *Healing Damaged Emotions* to start.

As quickly as you're able, get back to a normal routine, but don't push it. You're not unusual or stupid if you have a flashback. Even if you don't understand your feelings — accept them.

Most important, look to Jesus. Remember what the psalmist said: "Cast your burden upon the LORD, and He will sustain you; He will never allow the righteous to be shaken" (Psalm 55:22, NASB).

God will heal you and set you free.

ACTION SECTION

1. Which, if any, of these problems is the most significant for you personally?

———— Pornography   ———— Homosexuality

———— Oral Sex   ———— Sexual Abuse

———— Sexually Transmitted   ———— Rape
Diseases

2. For you to experience healing from the wounds of your problem, follow these practical steps of action. If you do, you will be on the road to recovery. Fill out your answers on a separate sheet of paper.

(1) *Realize how this problem has affected you.* To

deal with it completely, you need to be brutally honest. Don't try to hide anything. Write down what you're feeling.

(2) *Repent of your sin.* Get before God and admit your sin and guilt, whether it's the act itself or hatred toward someone who violated you. Tell Him that you want to get out of the problem. Turn the problem, and everything associated with it, over to God. You must be willing to cut off everything in the past that has gotten you into this problem. (For example, toss any pornography in the dumpster.) Write out your prayer of repentance.

(3) *Recognize your need for deliverance.* Possibly this problem has given sin such a grip on your life that you feel like you can't break free. But there is a way to break free — ask God to release sin's hold on you. Read 2 Corinthians 10:4,5, and get with an older, mature Christian. Ask God to deliver you from sin's grasp. Pray together, claiming the power of the name of Jesus and His blood shed on the cross. Pray until you know that you've confessed all sin in this area and feel peace in your heart that you've been released. If you think you need professional help with this, discuss it first with your parents (if possible), and then see your pastor.

(4) *Receive God's love.* He loves you and He wants His love to overwhelm you and heal you. Picture yourself being washed (taking a shower) in God's love. Study Romans 8:31-39 until you know that God's love for you will overcome your past. Pray to Jesus to let His love flow over you, to cleanse you. Ask Him to let you experience the reality of Romans 5:8. Write that prayer now.

(5) *Renew your mind.* As you saturate your mind with Jesus' words, you will discover the reality of Romans 12:1,2 — you will be transformed into the person God created you to be. That transformation will take place as you read, study and memorize God's Word. You will then make those tough decisions to obey God's Word, regardless of your feelings or desires. Write out what you plan to do every day to renew your mind.

(6) *Share your burden with a mature Christian.* Find

an older Christian of the same sex who you can trust, and tell that person all you are going through. Ask him (or her) these five questions:

1. I have a problem with _____ . Will you help me?
2. After I tell you the background, will you help me discover the root cause?
3. Will you pray for the Lord to set me free from this situation?
4. Will you help me see a professional counselor, if we agree that I need one?
5. Will you hold me accountable to grow as a Christian and get involved in a church where I can grow?

3. Write the name of the person you will talk to about your problem. _____

Why have you selected that person?_____

_____

_____

_____

4. If you think you need professional help, who will you see? _____

Make sure he or she is a Christian.

5. To get more insight on the solution process offered here, read chapter 12, "How Do I Get Control?"

11

How Do I Straighten Out the Past? ♥

W hen I walk down the hall at school and I see my ex-girlfriend I feel so guilty. I can't even look her in the eye." (An eighteen-year-old guy.)

"Guilt surrounds me. I am trapped. I have not been pure. My boyfriend and I have gone too far. We want to go back, but we can't. How can I get rid of the guilt of my past? I want to get my life together, but right now I'm miserable. Help!" (A seventeen-year-old girl.)

Sex in a relationship is fragile. When you mess up sexually, the whole relationship gets messed up. Relationships are like a ball of string — one moment it's a nice, neat ball, the next moment, because of your actions, it's all tangled up. Now it seems impossible to get all of the knots and tangles out. Is there any way to straighten out the mess you have made in your relationships?

Yes! But it takes a radical change in your thoughts

159

and actions. That will be painful. The apostle Paul said, "So I always take *pains* to have a clear conscience toward God and toward men" (Acts 24:16, RSV, italics added). Notice the word *pains*. Getting relationships straightened out means breaking off some relationships, dealing honestly with the past, healing your wounds, cleaning up your conscience and overhauling your mind. If you're ready for that, you can get your relationships straightened out.

You may see only the one relationship between you and your boyfriend/girlfriend that needs help, but to truly straighten out your past, *three* relationships need to get untangled.

YOUR RELATIONSHIP WITH GOD

After we finished speaking to a group of students, a beautiful gal came up and, with great pain, told us how she had gone to a party and was offered a drink. She had never had a drink before, but she took it. Then she took another one. After three or four, she was drunk. Then the guy she was with had sex with her. She got pregnant. Not knowing what to do, she had an abortion. Her life fell apart. She said, "I don't know what to do; I feel so dirty. Is there any hope for me?"

This story is just one of thousands, each with a personal, painful twist. God has both bad news and good news for you.

The Bad News

Look at what you have done. Isaiah describes it clearly: "We all, like sheep, have gone astray, each of us has turned to his own way" (Isaiah 53:6). The apostle Paul expresses it this way: "Don't be misled; remember that you can't ignore God and get away with it: a man will always reap just the kind of crop he sows" (Galatians 6:7, TLB).

God's law is this:

You reap what you sow.
You reap more than you sow.

You reap later than you sow.

You sowed bad choices all along the way, and now you're living with a harvest of guilt.

You're heartsick that you went beyond your limits, lost your virginity, got pregnant, or had an abortion. More important, you have sinned against God. *In no way* can you have a close relationship with Him in your condition.

That sounds harsh. And it is. Not because God is mean, but because that's what sin does. Do you see what your sin does? If you look at it honestly, it's enough to make you sick. You can do only one thing about it: Repent. That does not mean that you are sorry you got caught, or that you feel bad because you are guilty. Rather it means you turn away from your past behavior and turn totally to Jesus Christ. Give your life completely to Him, realizing that you can't run it yourself. Are you willing to do that?

The Good News

When you repent, God comes to you and pours His amazing love on you. Even though Jesus hates what you have done, *He loves you!* Isaiah 53:4,5 (NKJ) shows you how great that love is:

> Surely He has borne our griefs and carried our sorrows; yet we esteemed Him stricken, smitten by God, and afflicted. But He was wounded for our transgressions, He was bruised for our iniquities; the chastisement for our peace was upon Him.

Jesus Christ carried your sin on His shoulders. "Surely He has borne our griefs and carried our sorrows" (verse 4). When you messed up, you felt you had the weight of the world on your shoulders. But Jesus is right there to carry the heavy burden of what you did on *His* shoulders.

Jesus Christ hurt for you. "But He was wounded for our transgressions [sins], He was bruised for our iniquities" (verse 5). Jesus understands your hurt. He felt every bit of the hurt you have felt. Far beyond that, He took all your

hurt on the cross when He died. He took on your hurt so
you would not have to bear it.

Jesus Christ forgives your sin. "The chastisement
[punishment] for our peace was upon Him" (verse 5). Because of what Jesus did on the cross, when you give Him
control of your life, you are not punished for what you did
wrong. Jesus takes that on Himself. God doesn't hold your
sin over you. Isaiah expressed it another way: "Come now,
let us reason together, says the LORD. Though your sins are
like scarlet, they shall be as white as snow; though they are
red as crimson, they shall be like wool" (Isaiah 1:18).

Jesus Christ heals you. "By His stripes we are
healed" (verse 5). Because of the nightmare of the cross,
what you did no longer needs to be a nightmare to you.
Your life doesn't need to be destroyed. In fact Jesus will
completely heal you, putting all the pieces back together to
make you whole. He will use this weakness in your life to
reach others who need to hear about His love.

Isn't that amazing? Only Jesus can do that, because
He died on the cross and rose again from the grave three
days later. His love and power are so great that He can give
you a gift that no amount of money can buy — *spiritually
restored virginity.*

Picture God looking out of heaven through a microscope at you — your life is on a biology slide under the
microscope. He sees all of the bad things you have ever
done, including when you messed up sexually. Then you in-
vited Jesus into your life and turned from your sin. Now all
God sees is Jesus Christ in you, and Jesus is perfect! Because Jesus lives in you, God sees you just like His Son:
perfect.

The apostle Paul explains how God restores your
virginity spiritually: "He [God] chose us in Him [Christ], before the foundation of the world, that we should be holy and
blameless before Him" (Ephesians 1:4, NASB). WOW!
When God looks at you, all He sees is that you are "holy
and blameless" — in the right relationship with God.

Perhaps you're thinking, *What about my sin?* Ephesians 1:7,8 says:

> So overflowing is his kindness towards us that he took away all our sins through the blood of his Son, by whom we are saved; and he has showered down upon us the richness of his grace — for how well he understands us and knows what is best for us at all times (TLB).

WOW! No matter how badly you sinned or how many times, Jesus offers you the gift of total forgiveness and total healing — spiritually restored virginity.

There is only one way to have this gift. Receive it. First John 1:9 tells how: "If we confess our sins, he is faithful and just and will forgive us our sins and purify us from all unrighteousness."

Right now, pray this prayer of confession to straighten out your relationship with God:

> Lord Jesus, I have messed up my sex life. I admit that I sinned against You when I did that. I have messed up my relationship with You. My life is all tangled up, and You are the only one who can straighten it out. I turn away from my sin. I hate it. I give it to You completely. Right now I receive Your love and forgiveness. I am no longer dirty, sinful and guilty. I am clean, holy and blameless because of Jesus Christ. Thank You for the precious gift of spiritually restoring my virginity. In Jesus' name, Amen.

YOUR RELATIONSHIP WITH YOURSELF

Another time when we were speaking, a student told us, "I understand what Jesus did for me, and I accept that. But I still feel guilty. And that guilt hangs over me like a cloud."

It's one thing to have a clear conscience with God, but quite another to have your mind and emotions free from the guilt your sin produced. Again, we have bad news and good news.

The Bad News

Your "guilt gauge" is broken. In other words, your conscience isn't working. Either you feel no guilt at all (or very little) or you feel too much guilt. Like a broken thermometer which shows the wrong temperature, your conscience isn't serving you well.

At each point in your progress toward sexual involvement, you became less and less sensitive to your conscience, so your "guilt gauge" went lower and lower until it broke. Now you don't know whether you have true guilt or false guilt. So you either get depressed or you change your standards to convince yourself that what you're doing is not really wrong. When you are confronted about your behavior, you say, "I know what I'm doing." You compromise more and more sexually. If you continue, you eventually become convinced that free sex is the only way to go. The good becomes bad and the bad becomes good.[1]

Once you turn to Christ and receive His love and forgiveness, the facts of your relationship with God are right, but your guilt feelings are still messed up. Your "guilt gauge" is out of whack. That's bad news.

The Good News

You can get rid of your guilt.

Decide whether it's true or false guilt. God gave you a conscience to make you feel guilty when you do something wrong. But when your "guilt gauge" gets broken, you'll feel guilty even when you're not.

False guilt sounds like this:

- "You're a failure."
- "I told you so."
- "You're worthless."

If you are "in Christ" — Christ lives in you — the Bible promises that He doesn't condemn you. Romans 8:1 says, "Therefore, there is now no condemnation for those who are in Christ Jesus." So only two options exist for the guilt you feel.

First option: Your guilt is the conviction of the Holy Spirit. The Holy Spirit shows you that you are guilty, challenges you to be honest about it, causes you to bring your sin to Christ for forgiveness and then restores your joy.

Second option: Your guilt is the condemnation of Satan. If it is not Christ who is convicting you, then it is Satan condemning you. That condemnation leads to confusion, frustration, despair, hopelessness and separation from God. Satan's condemnation causes you to blame yourself. False guilt is Satan's way of putting distance between you and God and hindering your spiritual growth. Reject false guilt.

Now that you're right with God, your "guilt gauge" is fixed. Your mind and conscience will only make you feel guilty when you do something wrong. It won't condemn you or tell you that you're a failure. Rather it will cause you to turn to Jesus to seek His forgiveness.

Forgive yourself. Make a list of everything from your past that condemns you. Pray about every item on your list. Accept the fact that "God did not send his Son into the world to condemn the world, but to save the world through him. Whoever believes in him is not condemned" (John 3: 17,18a). Thank God that the blood of Jesus Christ has covered your sins and that you are free from them — no longer condemned, no longer guilty, but completely forgiven. Then tear up the list and throw it away as a symbol of what God has done for you.

Love yourself. Jesus died on the cross for you — He thinks you are worth loving. Not only does God love you, but He also wants you to love yourself. The second greatest commandment is to "love your neighbor as you love yourself" (see Matthew 22:36-38). Before you can love the people around you, you have to be able to love yourself. If the guilt keeps plaguing you, and you know Jesus has forgiven you, tell God out loud every day: "I am worth loving because Jesus Christ died for me and lives in me. I am special because You created me and love me." Read Bible passages like John 3:16-21, John 15:9, Romans 8:31-39, 1

John 4:7-21.

Open up to someone else. Find someone of the same sex and more mature in their relationship with Christ and tell them what you think and feel. You might think, "They'll reject me," but that's not true. That person will love you and respect you for being so open. James 5:16 says, "Confess your sins to each other and pray for each other so that you may be healed." You'll be amazed at how much strength and freedom you'll receive by opening up like this.

Settle only for total victory. In getting rid of sexual sin, people think they will get rid of it "once and for all." They can, but it takes time, perseverance and relying on the Holy Spirit. Never accept sin or treat it lightly. From time to time, however, you may give in to the temptation. If you do, God does not condemn you; rather, He is your lawyer to declare you "not guilty." The apostle John tells us: "My dear children, I write this to you so that you will not sin. But if anybody does sin, we have one who speaks to the Father in our defense — Jesus Christ, the Righteous One. He is the atoning sacrifice for our sins, and not only for ours but also for the sins of the whole world" (1 John 2:1,2).

Don't dwell on your sin and failures, but focus on the progress you're making toward total victory.

Now you can wake up every morning and realize that no matter what has happened in the past, you can say, "Because God loves me, I can love myself."

YOUR RELATIONSHIP WITH THE OTHER PERSON

One student put his need to apologize for the past this way: "I know what I did was wrong, and I want to be able to look that girl in the eye again — but I don't know what to do or what to say."

You probably have a hard time facing up to this, too. So how do you go about getting the relationship straightened out? Another bad news/good news explanation will help you see how it works.

The Bad News

When you go too far, one or both of you has been violated. That brings hurt feelings, tears, anger, resentment and bitterness. As one girl said, "It hurts so bad. I hate him."

In addition to the lack of trust and respect which we described earlier, here are other painful problems caused by premarital sex.

Communication breakdown. Once you go beyond your limits, it's amazing how much time and energy you spend talking and arguing about it. You no longer have "fun" conversations or talks about the Lord. You are consumed with your physical involvement.

Relationship breakup. When you go too far you only have two options: (1) break up and start over; or (2) go farther. The first is almost impossible, so you go farther.

When your relationship gets more intense you only have two options: (1) get married; or (2) break up. The first option is absurd and so you break up. You don't want to. You care for each other, but you fight all the time. A fantastic relationship — smashed.

Marriage wipeout. Your hopes and dreams of a wonderful marriage are wiped out when you compromise physically. Your physical involvement is creating tremendous problems for your future marriage. You open the gift of sex now, instead of later — and probably with someone you will never marry. Later, you have deep regret.

Spiritual dropout. Although you may still be involved in church activities, all you think about is your dating relationship — either how good or how bad it is. The guilt is affecting you so strongly that you can't concentrate on knowing God. When you have your eyes focused so intensely on the physical relationship, there is no way you can put Jesus in first place in your life.

All of these problems bring real pain. The relationship is wiped out — all for a sexual thrill. So what can you do to make the relationship right again?

The Good News

God has provided a way for you to get your past and present relationships straightened out. It happens by asking forgiveness. Forgiveness is God's powerful tool to untangle messed-up relationships. In order to use it, you will have to drop your pride, tell God that you will be totally obedient, and pray for courage. It's easy to say, "It's no big deal" — but it is. Don't back out. God wants you to follow through.

Jesus tells you how: "Therefore, if you are offering your gift at the altar and there remember that your brother has something against you, leave your gift there in front of the altar. First go and be reconciled to your brother; then come and offer your gift" (Mattthew 5:23,24). Jesus is speaking of a relationship in which you have wronged another person. He gives you three steps to make the relationship right: (1) remember, (2) reconcile, and (3) return.

Remember. Jesus said, "If you are offering your gift at the altar and there *remember* that your brother has something against you . . ." (Matthew 5:23).

Think for a moment. Who have you used sexually? Who have you hurt because of your selfish sexual desires? It's not hard to come up with a list. God will bring those people to mind. Be honest. Don't leave someone off because you're afraid to talk to him or her. Don't blame the other person, but take the responsibility yourself, even though the other person may have gone along with your actions.

Reconcile. Jesus said, "Leave your gift there in front of the altar. First go and be *reconciled* to your brother" (Matthew 5:24).

The word *reconcile* means to put back into a right relationship. You need to take two steps to be reconciled:

1. Confess your sin to God. Take each one of the people on your list to the Lord. Talk to Him about them. Confess to Him what you have done. Then know that God has forgiven you for that sin. His promise in 1 John 1:9 is true for you (read that verse again now). You are clean before God!

2. Confess your sin to the other person. To do that,

write out exactly what you want to say before you go. Avoid using terms like "I apologize," or "I was wrong but..." Instead, use these words:

- "I was wrong in the way I treated you in our relationship."
- "Here is how I was wrong." (Tell specifically what you did.)
- "Will you forgive me?"

When you do this, talk to the person *face to face*. Don't write a letter. Call only if the person is so far away that you can't meet in person.

When you get together, do so in a neutral, unromantic place. In the emotion of getting the friendship back together, there will be sexual temptation. Don't give in or you will be in a bigger mess than before. If this appears to be a problem, take a friend along who will wait outside for you.

Return. Jesus said, "Then come and offer your gift" (Matthew 5:24). Now that you know you have done everything possible to make the relationship right, you can return to God's presence with a clean conscience. You can put it behind you. Psalm 103:12 promises that "as far as the east is from the west, so far has he removed our transgressions from us." In order to make sure that it is behind you . . .

- Let go of any false guilt you are carrying about the past. God has set you free from that.
- Don't allow the other person's response determine whether you're forgiven or not. If that person forgives you — great. But what if he or she gets even angrier and does not forgive you? You have done all you can to make the relationship right. Getting the relationship right is no longer your responsibility. Just make sure that now you don't hold a grudge against that person for not forgiving you.
- Continue to pray for that person.

WHEN SOMEONE HURTS YOU

God has given you a way to take care of your hurts, too. For that to happen you must be willing to let God heal your pain. That's not easy, because with the hurt comes anger, resentment and bitterness that can eat you up.

If someone has hurt you, Jesus gives you the steps to make that relationship right again in Matthew 18:15-17.

Release Your Resentment

Jesus said, "If your brother sins against you, go and show him his fault, just between the two of you" (Matthew 18:15). Jesus *doesn't* mean to go and blast that person out of the water.

Jesus wants you to deal with *your* hurts first. He gives a principle for that in Matthew 7:3: "Why do you look at the speck of sawdust in your brother's eye and pay no attention to the plank in your own eye?" The "plank" in your eye is your bitter attitude toward the other person for what he or she has done to you. Jesus says you've got to get that plank out of your eye — you've got to deal with your attitude.

- Tell God how you feel about all that has happened. Be honest with Him. He can take it.
- Confess all of the hurt, anger, resentment and bitterness to Him. Ask Him to forgive you for your attitude. Even though it was the other person who hurt you, admit that you did not respond correctly. Thank God for His promise in 1 John 1:9. Read that and let it sink in.
- Ask Jesus to heal those hurts and make you whole. Mention each hurt to Him and picture His love soothing those hurts and making them well.

Right the Relationship

Jesus said, "Go and show him his fault" (Matthew 18:15). How can you get the relationship right? Pray for that person until all of your emotions are under control. Then write out exactly what you want to say before you go. Use these words:

- "I have been wrong in my attitude toward you."
- "You hurt me deeply. (Tell how that person hurt you.) But I responded in the wrong way."
- "Will you forgive me for my wrong attitude toward you?"

Rebuild Your Relationship

Jesus said, "If he listens to you, you have won your brother over" (Matthew 18:15). You can "win your brother" and rebuild your friendship. To rebuild that friendship:

Decide. Since you are the one who was hurt, you must decide if you want to be friends. In the relationship there has probably been fighting, arguing, very little understanding of feelings, and selfishness. You have gotten hurt in that. Do you want to be a friend? Consider Proverbs 17:17 in your decision: "A friend loves at all times."

Discuss. Openly discuss your relationship face to face. Be very clear that this is not for romance, but friendship.

Pray. Together ask God to overcome your past and build your friendship for the future.

Counsel. Seek the counsel of an adult if you run into a snag and can't restore the friendship. Matthew 18:16 says, "But if he will not listen, take one or two others along, so that 'every matter may be established by the testimony of two or three witnesses.'"

Quit. If any romantic feelings get involved in the relationship again, then quit hanging around with each other. One mistake is enough.

If you follow through on the advice in this chapter, you can leave the past in the past. Once you have gotten your relationships right, move on toward the future: "Brothers, I do not consider myself yet to have taken hold of it. But one thing I do: Forgetting what is behind and straining toward what is ahead, I press on toward the goal to win the prize for which God has called me heavenward in Christ Jesus" (Philippians 3:13,14). Get the past straight, then press on!

ACTION SECTION

If you have become involved sexually, or gone beyond your limits, think through the following:

1. *In your relationship with God*, describe how Jesus Christ has taken care of your sexual sin and given you *spiritually restored virginity.*

_____

_____

_____

2. *In your relationship with yourself,* what specific steps will you take from the chapter to fix your "guilt gauge" and to love yourself?

_____

_____

_____

3. *In your relationship with the other person*, write what you will do and what you will say to the person you hurt.

_____

_____

_____

4. Write down what you will do and say to the person who hurt you.

_____

_____

_____

12

How Do I Get Control? ♥

What is your room like? Picture it in your mind. Is it messy? How messy?

Imagine that six months ago your mom, in no uncertain terms, told you that she was not going to clean your room under any circumstance. And she hasn't. So now you don't just walk into your room — you shove the door open and *climb* into it. A note from the Environmental Protection Agency announces a quarantine on your room because of the toxic fumes created by your unwashed clothes. The dust balls under your bed have turned into a dust blob, and it's swallowing everything.

It's been six months since you changed your sheets, and now something is growing on them. When you sleep, this fungus (or whatever it is) tickles your back.

Garbage is everywhere — and it seems to be growing out of your trash can. Four months ago you had a "Big Mac

Attack," and when you finished you threw the remains toward the trash can. Now there is a pickle on the rim of the can that has mold all around it. Three months ago you ordered in a pizza. When you tossed the leftovers toward the trash can, a piece of pepperoni stuck to the wall. The roaches and ants are having a tug-of-war for it.

Your room is definitely not under control. You're saying "This is gross. It's out of control. Get the garbage out." Since Mom isn't taking the trash out anymore, the only way to get it done is to take it out yourself.

Your life can get as messy as your room. Trashy thoughts develop into immoral actions and habits that cause your sex life to get out of control. What you need to know now is how to get the trash out of your life, and keep it out, so you can be the clean, pure person God designed you to be.

In order to discover how to get control, focus on 2 Timothy 2:20-22:

> In a large house there are articles not only of gold and silver, but also of wood and clay; some are for noble purposes and some for ignoble. If a man cleanses himself from the latter, he will be an instrument for noble purposes, made holy, useful to the Master and prepared to do any good work. Flee the evil desires of youth, and pursue righteousness, faith, love and peace, along with those who call on the Lord out of a pure heart.

As Paul writes to Timothy he tells him that there are only two kinds of containers ("articles") — impure and pure. One is a trash can, the other is a temple. Which one are you?

THE TRASH CAN — IMPURE

See how much your life relates to this common experience:

> In junior high I began to take the words written on the bathroom and locker room walls and use them in my vocabulary. About that same time I started the junior-high party

scene, playing smacky-face and huggy-poo. In high school I moved on to heavier stuff. The make-out scene got hot and heavy with Roto-Rooter kisses. Masturbation was a constant issue.

The garbage gets piled up. One man relates a painful lesson:

When I got married, I thought that all my problems with immoral thoughts and actions were solved. It was all taken care of, right? Wrong! Have you ever heard the phrase "dirty old man"? Well a dirty old man starts out as a dirty *young* man! If you have trash in your mind when you're young, you'll have that trash when you're older. Getting married doesn't change that. I woke up one day and realized that my mind was a trash can.

Titus 1:15-16 lists the ways to know if you are impure:

To the pure, all things are pure, but to those who are corrupted and do not believe, their minds and consciences are corrupted. They claim to know God, but by their actions they deny him. They are detestable, disobedient and unfit for doing anything good.

These verses reveal five ways to measure your trash level.

Trash Level Test

On a scale of 1 to 5, where are you?

1. Are your mind and conscience corrupted? (That means you have an X-rated mind now and things in your past that you hope no one ever finds out.)

1	2	3	4	5
Yes				No

2. Do you profess to know God, but deny Him by your deeds? (That means you talk a big game at church, but

on Saturday night it's a different story.)

1   2   3   4   5
Yes   No

3. Are you detestable? (That means you are obnoxious in the way you treat the opposite sex.)

1   2   3   4   5
Yes   No

4. Are you disobedient to your parents? (That means you do your own thing regardless of how your parents feel about who you should date and what you should do on a date.)

1   2   3   4   5
Yes   No

5. Are you unfit for any good deed? (That means that you are so into yourself that you can't think of anybody else. You try to satisfy your own selfish sexual desires.)

1   2   3   4   5
Yes   No

Be honest! You may have impurity in your life. You have put garbage in and now garbage is coming out. Now you desperately need the solution to get the trash out and gain control of your thoughts and desires.

How can you become pure?

THE TEMPLE — PURE

You can clean out the trash can and let Jesus take control so your body can become "the temple of the Holy Spirit" (see 1 Corinthians 3:16). Take action on 2 Timothy 2:22: "Flee the evil desires of youth, and pursue righteousness, faith, love and peace, along with those who call on the Lord out of a pure heart."

Paul gives three powerful decisions that must be made if you are going to be pure.

Decision One: Flee Evil Desires

Another word for *evil desires* is "passions." The word *passions* means lusts, cravings, passionate desires. How do you get that passion under control? Paul says to "flee" from it. How do you do that?

Run with your body. As a follower of Jesus Christ, you are in a race. You are running away from your passions and toward Jesus Christ. The writer of Hebrews puts it this way: "Therefore, since we are surrounded by such a great cloud of witnesses, let us throw off everything that hinders and the sin that so easily entangles, and let us run with perseverance the race marked out for us" (Hebrews 12:1).

You know that you can't run fast if you have your warm-ups on and a barbell in your gym bag. But how about relating that to your sex life? Will you lay aside the warm-up suit of impurity and the barbell of sexual sin that clings to you and weighs you down? This is a significant decision you have to make *now*. Which of these weights do you need to lay aside?

_____ Having lustful thoughts
_____ Looking at lust-producing material
_____ Engaging in masturbation
_____ Giving in to pressure
_____ Going too far—beyond my personal limits
_____ Having sexual intercourse

These are some of the weights you'll need to throw off if you want to run with Christ. Throw them off now.

It's also important that you run in the right direction at the right time. Let's say you're on a date with a person you have wanted to go out with for a long time. At six o'clock you were anticipating a fantastic evening, but now it's 10:30 and you're all alone together in the car, steaming up the windows. Suddenly you realize you have gone further than you wanted to. You want to say "STOP!" and you want to run. That takes tremendous energy and courage in the heat of the situation. When most couples get that far they do whatever comes naturally.

But watch this! How much better it would have been to say "STOP" and to have run *earlier* in the evening. You could have done that . . .

- when you got into the car and scooted real close to each other;
- when you decided not to go to the game as origi- nally planned but to drive around instead;
- when your date suggested you go out to where your friends park — just to see who's there;
- when you parked the car;
- when you kissed the first time.

After that point, you had a marathon race staring you in the face! You could have run by saying:

- "I enjoy being close to you, but I need a little space. Besides, when I get close to people, I sweat."
- "I would prefer to go to the game."
- "All of our friends are at the game. They'll miss seeing us."
- "If I stay in a car too long I get carsick. In fact if we're going to stay here, I feel sick already. Could we go to my house?"
- "I know the Lord Jesus Christ doesn't want me to do this. So let's stop now."

Take the early opportunities. It makes the run much easier.

Decision Two: Aim at Jesus Christ

Second Timothy 2:22 says to "pursue righteousness, faith, love and peace." And who are those the qualities of? Jesus Christ! In this race to become pure, He is the finish line — the goal toward whom you are aiming.

The apostle Paul talks about reaching the goal like this: "Brethren . . . one thing I do, forgetting what lies behind and striving toward what lies ahead, I press on toward the goal for the prize of the upward call of God in Christ Jesus"

(Philippians 3:13,14, RSV). To aim at Jesus Christ, you must first take care of the past so you won't keep looking back. (If you are still looking back, go through chapter 11 again carefully, taking action on each point before going any further.) Then "press on toward the goal."

A friend used this intriguing phrase to advertise a meeting for students in his city: "Come and see the world's most powerful sex organ." Students came from all over the city. As you can imagine, there was a great sense of excitement. On the stage our friend had a table on either side of him, each with a large sack — one labeled "His" and one labeled "Hers." With great fanfare he opened the bags and pulled out "The world's most powerful sex organ": a brain.

See, it's not your body or your sex organs that determine your sex life — it's your mind. In Romans 8:5,6 Paul explains: "Those who live according to the sinful nature have their minds set on what that nature desires; but those who live in accordance with the Spirit have their minds set on what the Spirit desires. The mind of sinful man is death, but the mind controlled by the Spirit is life and peace."

Everyone who has Jesus Christ living in them can "live in accordance with the Spirit." And those who live according to the Spirit don't set their minds on the flesh (trash), but on the things of the Spirit (temple). You must set your mind!

But you say, "My mind is so messed up. I have such dirty, impure thoughts." How do you keep the world (peer pressure) from squeezing you into its mold? How can your life be transformed (changed) to be like the life of Jesus Christ? The apostle Paul puts it this way in Romans 12:2: "Do not conform any longer to the pattern of this world, but be transformed by the renewing of your mind."

Ralph Waldo Emerson said, "You are what you think about." One guy commented, "If that were totally true, I'd be a basketball or a girl." Philippians 4:8 gives direction to Emerson's statement: "Finally, brothers, whatever is true, whatever is noble, whatever is right, whatever is pure, whatever is lovely, whatever is admirable — if anything is excellent or praiseworthy — *think about such things.*"

Three actions will help you set your mind on Jesus Christ.

Praise the Lord. Guys, when you see a sexy girl walking down the hall, look away and praise the Lord. Or girls, when you get excited when "The Hunk" is around, praise the Lord. The Scriptures instruct us to praise the Lord in everything. That's definitely in the category of everything, isn't it? But why "praise the Lord"?

- To express that Jesus Christ made you pure. When you accepted Christ, He made you pure whether you act like it or not. Ephesians 1:4 says you are "holy and blameless."
- To affirm your healthy sexual desires. Remember He made you. For you to appreciate the opposite sex is natural. You can praise Him and thank Him for that.
- To express trust in God. You can trust Him because one day He will give you a husband or wife toward whom you can direct all of your sexual desires and not feel the least bit guilty.
- To change your focus. Instead of looking at your needs or at the other person, you look toward God Himself. When your focus is on Him, He can control your thoughts.
- To bring Jesus into every situation.

When you praise the Lord, your mind will be set on Jesus.

Memorize Scripture. Minds are like tape recorders. They record any thought that goes into them. That information is stored in your brain over the years. If you are going to renew your mind, to change it from a trash can into a temple, you have to stop thinking *your* thoughts and start thinking *God's* thoughts.

In order to think God's pure thoughts, instead of your own impure thoughts, you have to have His thoughts in your mind. If you are like the average person, once you get past

John 3:16 and "Jesus wept" you probably don't have much of the Bible in your mind. But memorizing Scripture helps you keep your life pure. The psalmist said it this way: "How can a young man [or woman] keep his way pure? By living according to your word. I seek you with all my heart; do not let me stray from your commands. I have hidden your word in my heart that I might not sin against you" (Psalm 119:9-11). It's not the dusty Bible on your desk but the Word of God hidden in your heart that will change your life!

So guys, when you are lying on the bed at night with that picture of a girl in your mind, and girls, when you start to fantasize about a guy, here's what you do after you praise the Lord. You bring to mind verses you have memorized, like Psalm 119:9-11 above and others:

- Philippians 4:8   "Finally, brothers, whatever is true, whatever is noble, whatever is right, whatever is pure, whatever is lovely, whatever is admirable — if anything is excellent or praiseworthy — think about such things."

- Philippians 4:13   "I can do everything through him who gives me strength."

- 1 Corinthians 10:13 "No temptation has seized you except what is common to man. And God is faithful; he will not let you be tempted beyond what you can bear. But when you are tempted, he will also provide a way out so that you can stand up under it."

- Hebrews 2:18   "Because he himself suffered when he was tempted, he is able to help those who are being tempted."

- Hebrews 4:15   "For we do not have a high priest who is unable to sympathize with our weaknesses, but

we have one who has been
tempted in every way, just as we
are — yet was without sin."

That replaces your thoughts with God's thoughts.
Then "the world's most powerful sex organ" will neutralize
your sexual desires and change the way you think. (For more
help on memorizing Scripture, see page 109.)

Picture Jesus. Your mind is not only like a tape
recorder but also like a camera — it takes pictures of everything it sees. When you see a sexy girl or an attractive man,
your mind takes a snapshot of that. At night, when you are
lying in bed, your mind brings out the photo album and begins to look at the pictures. What do you do?

You get a new roll of film and take different pictures.
Take pictures based on Colossians 3:1-3:

> Since, then, you have been raised with Christ, set
> your hearts on things above, where Christ is seated at the right
> hand of God. Set your minds on things above, not on earthly
> things. For you died, and your life is now hidden with Christ
> in God.

Paul tells you to seek (take pictures of) the things that
are above. Who is there? Jesus Christ. What is He doing?
He's seated at God's right hand. Take a picture of Jesus
Christ — on His throne! Take a picture of Him on the cross,
taking all of your sins on Himself. Take a picture of Him at
the resurrection bursting out of the tomb to give you new
life. Take a picture of Him living inside of you, controlling
your life. WOW! What a roll of pictures!

Only Jesus can make you pure. And as you praise
the Lord, memorize Scripture, and picture Jesus, there is no
question that He will change your mind. He will transform
you from a trash can into a temple.

Decision Three: Make New Friends

Back in 2 Timothy 2:22 Paul says that the third step
to get control is to get new friends. He says when you flee

evil desires and aim at Jesus Christ, you do that "along with those who call upon the Lord for a pure heart." In other words, you need to have friends who are pure.

If you're hanging around with people who are impure, they will pull you into the trash can with them. Your desire is to be pure, but your friends keep pulling you down. Take two steps of action.

Find pure friends. That means quit hanging around with impure friends. Quit hanging around with friends who would rather be trash cans instead of temples. Don't just dump them, or be "holier than thou," but tell them you are committed to following Jesus Christ 100 percent. It's not that you'll never see them again — you should! But we're talking about the friends you spend time with regularly every day — your closest friends.

Start hanging around with pure friends. Look for at least one other person of the same sex who wants to be pure. Start hanging around with that person. Invite him or her to your house after school or to a school function. If you are wondering where to look for such a friend, try your church youth group or a group of Christians at school. (For more help on this, read our book *Love: Making It Last*.)

If your best friends are pure friends, God will use you and your friends to encourage each other. King Solomon said it this way: "Two are better than one, because they have a good return for their work: If one falls down, his friend can help him up. But pity the man who falls and has no one to help him up" (Ecclesiastes 4:9,10).

Date pure people. To break up with an impure boyfriend or girlfriend is a big step — and one of the hardest steps of all. Maybe, for you, the hardest yet. But it's absolutely necessary if you are going to be all God wants you to be.

The writer of Proverbs explains the consequences if you don't break up an impure relationship:

Young men, listen to me, and never forget what I'm about to say: Run from her! Don't go near her house, lest you

fall to her temptation and lose your honor, and give the re-
mainder of your life to the cruel and merciless; lest strangers
obtain your wealth, and you become a slave of foreigners.
Lest afterwards you groan in anguish and in shame, when
syphilis consumes your body, and you say, "Oh, if only I had
listened! If only I had not demanded my own way! Oh, why
wouldn't I take advice? Why was I so stupid? For now I
must face public disgrace" (Proverbs 5:7-14, TLB).

In order to know exactly what steps to take to break
up correctly, read chapter 11 in our book *Dating: Picking
(and Being) a Winner.*

Date only people who desire purity. That may mean
you won't date for a while. In order to know how to handle
waiting, read chapters 8 and 12 in *Dating.*

If you commit yourself to dating only those who want
to be pure, then the positive experience described by the
writer of Proverbs will be yours: "May your fountain be
blessed, and may you rejoice in the wife of your youth. A
loving doe, a graceful deer — may her breasts satisfy you
always, may you ever be captivated by her love" (Proverbs
5:18,19).

When you admit that you are impure and ask God to
make you pure through Jesus Christ, God can use you.
That's what 2 Timothy 2:21 says: "If a man cleanses himself
from the latter, he will be an instrument for noble purposes,
made holy, useful to the Master and prepared to do any good
work."

When you are pure, God can use you because you
are...

- a vessel — (a container);
- consecrated — (set apart);
- useful — (for service);
- ready — (right now).

Putting that together, you are a container set apart for
service right now.

You're thirsty so you go into your kitchen to get a
drink. On the counter is an expensive piece of crystal which

has been sitting there for three days. It contains three-day-old tea and an apple core, and there are lipstick stains around the rim. You look around and see a clean peanut butter jar in the cabinet. Which of the two are you going to use? That's obvious! And God is much smarter than you. He'll pick the clean container every time.

When your life is pure, it's under God's control. When it is under His control, He can use you.

If you're willing to take the steps to become a temple instead of a trash can, pray this prayer:

> Lord Jesus, I ask You to give me the honesty to confess that I have been impure. I pray for the strength to flee from evil desires, to aim at Jesus Christ and to get new friends. I will take each step of action in Your strength, not mine! Thank You that You make me pure through Jesus Christ. In His name, Amen.

As you live out what you've learned in this book, you will be prepared for sex in your marriage. And you'll not only *desire* the best sex life possible, but you'll *have* it. That will be awesome! While you're waiting, keep your eyes on Jesus!

ACTION SECTION

1. How did you score on the Trash Level Test on page 175?

25	Maybe you should write this book.
20 - 24	Definitely a temple; maintain your high standards.
15 - 19	You're making progress; work on the problem areas.
10 - 14	You're in the dangerous range; go through this chapter again and take action on every area needed.
5 - 9	Serious trouble; enlist help from your youth pastor.

What are the areas of impurity in your life? List them. (Be honest.)

_____

_____

_____

2. Check here whether or not you are 100 percent committed to purity.

_____ YES, 100 percent   _____ NO, not ready yet

Either way you answered, write your reasons.

_____

_____

_____

If You Want to Be Pure

3. From what situation is it the hardest for you to "flee evil desires" and run? _____

_____

_____

What will you do to run next time? Make a list of three practical steps.

(1)_____

(2)_____

(3)_____

4. Using the three practical suggestions given to "set your mind," how will you specifically apply each one to make you a temple?

Praise the Lord. _____

_____

Memorize Scripture. _____

_____

Picture Jesus. _____

_____

5. What action will you take to make new friends?

_____

_____

Who are the impure friends you'll stop spending most of your time with?

_____

_____

Do you need to break up with an impure boyfriend or girlfriend? Write specifically how you will do this.

_____

_____

5. Read *Dating: Picking (and Being) a Winner* to know how to pick a winner.

Notes

Introduction

1. Susanna McBee, "A Call to Tame the Genie of Sex," *U.S. News & World Report* (December 22, 1986), p. 8

Chapter 2

1. Josh McDowell and Paul Lewis, *Givers, Takers, and Other Kinds of Lovers* (Wheaton, IL: Tyndale House Publishers, 1980), p. 89.
2. Orlis J. Olson, *Sexuality: Guidelines for Teenagers* (Grand Rapids, MI: Baker Book House, 1981), pp. 19,22.
3. Dawson McAllister, *Discussion Manual for Student Relationships*, Volume 1 (Colorado: Roper Press, 1975), p. 112.

Chapter 3

1. John C. Souter, *Date* (Wheaton, IL: Tyndale House Publishers, 1986), p. 34.
2. Dawson McAllister, *Discussion Manual for Student Relationships*, Volume 1 (Colorado: Roper Press, 1975), p. 10.
3. Orlis J. Olson, *Sexuality: Guidelines for Teenagers* (Grand Rapids, MI: Baker Book House, 1981), n.p.
4. Taken from "The Christian and Sex," *Young Life Leadership Notes*, Mal McSwain, ed.

Chapter 4

1. Eric Sherman, "Teenage Sex—A Special Report," *Ladies Home Journal* (October 1986), p. 203.
2. Stacey and Paula Rinehart, *Choices* (Colorado Springs, CO: NavPress, 1982), p. 93.
3. Rinehart, *Choices*, pp. 92-93.
4. Ray E. Short, *Sex, Love or Infatuation* (Minneapolis, MN: Augsburg Publishing House, 1978), p. 45.
5. Tim Stafford, "Waiting for Love in a Hurry-Up World," *Campus Life* (May 1984), p. 34.
6. Fritz Rienecker, *Linguistic Key to the Greek New Testament* (Grand Rapids, MI: Regency Reference Library, 1976), p. 10.
7. W. E. Vine and Fleming Revell, *An Expository Dictionary of New Testament Words* (Westwood, NJ: Bethany House, 1940), p. 230.
8. Stafford, "Waiting for Love," p. 34.
9. Aaron Haas, *Teenage Sexuality: A Survey of Teenage Sexual Behavior* (Los Angeles, CA: Pinnacle Books, 1981), pp. 46-49.

Chapter 5

1. Scott Kirby, *Dating* (Grand Rapids, MI: Baker Book House, 1979), p. 77.
2. Tim Stafford, "Love, Sex and the Whole Person," *Campus Life* (May 1986), p. 14.
3. Rusty and Linda Wright, *Dynamic Sex* (San Bernardino, CA: Here's Life Publishers, 1979), p. 76.
4. Kirby, *Dating*, p. 77.
5. Kirby, *Dating*, pp. 77-78.
6. Wright, *Dynamic Sex*, p. 77.

7. Billy Beacham, *Growing in Godliness* (Fort Worth: Student Discipleship Ministries, 1986), p. 22.

Chapter 6
1. "Premarital Experience No Help in Sexual Adjustment After Marriage," *Family Life* (May 1972), pp. 1-2.
2. Aaron Haas, *Teenage Sexuality: A Survey of Teenage Sexual Behavior* (Los Angeles, CA: Pinnacle Books, 1981), pp. 46-49.
3. *Webster's New Collegiate Dictionary* (Springfield, MA: G. & C. Merriam Company, 1981), p. 1191.

Chapter 7
1. Aaron Haas as quoted by Jim Burns in *Handling Your Hormones* (Eugene, OR: Harvest House Publishers, 1978), pp. 125-26.
2. Coleen Kelly Mast, *Sex Respect: The Option of True Sexual Freedom* (Department of Health and Human Services, 1986), p. 20.
3. Larry Tomczak, "How to Win Over Sexual Sin and Have Victory," *People of Destiny* (March/April 1986), p. 5.
4. Thomas Schwartz, "How Far Is Too Far?" *Group* (August 1986), p. 10.
5. Several of the thoughts for this section are from Billy Beacham, *Growing in Godliness* (Fort Worth: International Evangelism Association, 1986), pp. 15,16.
6. Beacham, *Growing in Godliness*, p. 16.

Chapter 8
1. Jerry White, *Honesty, Morality and Conscience* (Colorado Springs, CO: NavPress, 1979), pp. 202-3.
2. Dr. George Statham, Decatur Pediatric Group, Atlanta, Georgia.
3. Jim Burns, *Handling Your Hormones* (Eugene, OR: Harvest House Publishers, 1986), p. 105.
4. White, *Honesty . . . Conscience*, pp. 203-4.
5. Randy Alcorn, *Christians in the Wake of the Sexual Revolution* (Portland, OR: Multnomah Press, 1985), p. 215.
6. Walter and Ingrid Trobisch, *My Beautiful Feeling* (Germany: Editions Trobisch, 1976), pp. 8-9.
7. John Catheros, "I'll Never Tell Anybody I Have a Problem With . . ." *People of Destiny* (March/April 1986), p. 27.

Chapter 9
1. "God's Answer for Teenage Sex," *Parents and Teenagers*, YFC Edition (Wheaton, IL: Scripture Press, 1985), p. 508.
2. "God's Answer for Teenage Sex," p. 508.
3. We recommend *The Financial Planning Workbook* by Larry Burkett (Chicago: Moody Press, 1982).
4. "The Value of Life," *Parents and Teenagers*, YFC Edition (Wheaton, IL: Scripture Press, 1985), p. 509.
5. Stavinlow Z. Leinbruch, M.D., "Fertility Problems Following Aborted First Pregnancy," *New Perspectives on Human Abortion*, Hilgers, Horan, Mall eds. (M. D. Frederick, University of Publications of America, 1981), pp. 120-34. And C. Medore,

et. al., "A Study on the Effect of Induced Abortion on Subsequent Pregnancy Outcome," (American Obstetrics and Gynecology, 1981), 139:516-21.

6. M. H. Liebman and J. S. Zimmer, "The Psychological Sequelae of Abortion: Fact and Fallacy," *Psychological Aspects of Abortion*, David Mall and Walter F. Watts, eds. (M. D. Frederick, University Publications of America, 1979), n.p.

7. Tamar Lewin, "Medical Use of Fetal Tissues Spurs New Abortion Debate," *New York Times* (August 18, 1987), p. A1.

8. Ed and Gaye Wheat, *Intended for Pleasure* (Old Tappan, NJ: Fleming H. Revell Company, 1977), pp. 202-3.

9. Coleen Kelly Mast, *Sex Respect: The Option of True Sexual Freedom* (Department of Health and Human Services, 1986), p. 48.

10. G. Keith Olson, *Counseling Teenagers* (Loveland, CO: Group Books, 1984), pp. 408-9.

11. Olson, *Counseling Teenagers*, p. 410.

12. Mast, *Sex Respect*, pp. 50-51.

Chapter 10

1. Aaron Haas, *Teenage Sexuality: A Survey of Teenage Sexual Behavior* (Los Angeles, CA: Pinnacle Books, 1981), p. 182.

2. Wendy Wertheimer of the American Social Health Association as quoted by Jean Seligmann in "A Nasty New Epidemic," *Newsweek* (February 4, 1985), p. 73.

3. The information for describing these diseases was taken from Scott St. Clair's research paper on the subject and Thomas Morris, "Venereal Disease: A Well-Kept Secret," *Parents and Teenagers* (Wheaton, IL: Scripture Press, 1984), pp. 511-15.

4. George Rekers, "When Homosexuality Tempts Children," *Moody* (June 1985), pp. 96-99.

5. Bob Sutton, "Homosexuality: A Problem the Church Can No Longer Keep Outside Its Walls," *New Wine* (June 1974), n.p.

6. Eloise Salholz, "Beware of the Child Molesters," *Newsweek* (August 9, 1982), p. 45.

7. Alice Huskey, "What You Need to Know About Sexual Abuse," *Youth Workers Journal* (Winter 1985), p. 66.

8. *Basic Facts About Child Abuse* (Chicago: National Committee for Prevention of Child Abuse, 1982), n.p.

9. G. Keith Olson, *Counseling Teenagers* (Loveland, CO: Group Books, 1984), pp. 435-36.

10. Shirley O'Brien, *Child Pornography* (Dubuque, IA: Tendall/Herst Publishing Co., 1983), p. 22.

11. Jim Burns, *Handling Your Hormones* (Eugene, OR: Harvest House Publishers, 1986), p. 123.

12. Olson, *Counseling Teenagers*, pp. 443-44.

13. Olson, *Counseling Teenagers*, pp. 444-45.

14. Deborah Roberts, *Raped* (Grand Rapids, MI: Zondervan, 1981), pp. 147-49. Used by permission.

Chapter 11

1. John C. Souter, "Steps to Moral Impurity," *Date* (May 1986), p. 39.

Handle
Your
Hassles!

Let popular youth speaker Bill Jones guide you through meaningful, contemporary Bible studies that help you succeed in life! These four-lesson studies are available now:

- *PARENTS: Raising Them Properly*
- *SELF-IMAGE: Learning to Like Yourself*
- *PEER PRESSURE: Standing Up For What You Believe*
- *TEMPTATION: Avoiding the Big Rip-Off*

And watch for more "Handling Your Hassles" studies to be published soon by Here's Life Publishers!

Available at your
Christian bookstore

Or call

Here's Life Publishers

Toll free 1-800-854-5659
In California call (714) 886-7981